D1093367

100 BOOKS EVERY FOLK MUSIC FAN SHOULD OWN

BEST MUSIC BOOKS

Lists abound for the best 100 songs or best 50 albums. But with so much fine writing and scholarship on music, how do we know which are the best books on jazz or rock 'n' roll or classical music? Contributions to **Best Music Books** provide definitive lists of those book-length works that every fan of any major musical genre should consider owning. Written by established experts in the field, each title offers summaries and evaluations of key works and their contribution to our understanding of today's many musical traditions.

100 Books Every Blues Fan Should Own by Edward Komara and Greg Johnson, 2014

100 Books Every Folk Music Fan Should Own by Dick Weissman, 2014

100 BOOKS EVERY FOLK MUSIC FAN SHOULD OWN

DICK WEISSMAN

ML128.F74 W45 2014
Weissman, Dick, author.
100 books every folk music
fan should own
Lanham, Maryland : Rowman &
Littlefield, [2014]

ROWMAN & LITTLEFIELD
Lanham • Boulder • New York • Toronto • Plymouth, UK

Published by Rowman & Littlefield
4501 Forbes Boulevard, Suite 200, Lanham, Maryland 20706
www.rowman.com

10 Thornbury Road, Plymouth PL6 7PP, United Kingdom

British Library Cataloguing in Publication Information Available

Library of Congress Cataloging-in-Publication Data
Weissman, Dick.
  100 books every folk music fan should own / Dick Weissman.
   pages cm. — (Best music books)
  Includes bibliographical references and index.
  ISBN 978-0-8108-8234-8 (cloth : alk. paper) — ISBN 978-0-8108-8666-7 (electronic) 1. Folk music—Bibliography. I. Title. II. Title: One hundred books every folk music fan should own.
  ML128.F74W45 2014
  016.78162'13—dc23

                                                          2013038345

Printed in the United States of America

To everyone who has played or thought
about American folk-based music

CONTENTS

THE 100 BOOKS
(AND THEN SOME)

Historical Surveys

Songbooks and Folk Song Collections

American Indians

The Immigrants

Spanish-Language Music in the United States

Politics, Protest and Workers' Songs, and the Folk Song Revival

Miscellaneous: A Little Bit of This and a Little Bit of That

Folk Rock and Freak Folk

The Business of Folk

Folk Instruments and Instructional Materials

Banjo

Dulcimer

Fiddle and Mandolin

ACKNOWLEDGMENTS

THANKS TO CHICO SCHWALL, FRIEND AND MULTI-INSTRUMEN-talist, for his advice on instructional materials. More thanks to Bennett Graff, the editor. The concept behind this book was his. I truly appreciate Michele Tomiak's careful copyediting.

Powell's Books and the Portland, Oregon, main library were great sources of books. I would also be remiss not to thank the many authors whose books I read, whether or not I included them in this volume.

INTRODUCTION

COMPILING THIS BOOK HAS BEEN QUITE AN ADVENTURE.
In 1976 I coauthored *The Folk Music Sourcebook* with Larry
Sandberg. My role was to do all of the book reviews while
Larry covered recordings. It was a formidable enough task
then, but since that time there has been a massive increase in
the literature of folk music. Instruction books, biographies,
autobiographies, songbooks, and histories of the folk music
revival have literally grown like weeds.

In compiling the list, I looked at a number of factors.
What makes a book more important than another book?
Sometimes it's the period when it was written, an original
approach to some aspect of folk music, a thorough study of an
area that hasn't been overly publicized or explored, or something that offers some special insights into the music or its
musicians. Sometimes a book made the list simply because no
one else has covered a particular subject at this time.

My book will inevitably be provocative. What seems important to one reader may seem insignificant to another. There
are many controversies in the folk music field. Who are the

key figures whose work is important? What musicians or subject areas are neglected or covered to the point of absurdity? Chances are that as you are reading this, yet another book about Bob Dylan has been published. This brings up another problem that I encountered in reading a number of books. Too many of the biographical works almost ignore music and focus on the subject's family history and an endless series of names and dates. I don't believe that it is necessary for a person writing about a musician to be a musicologist, but ignoring musical content is not really acceptable. On the other hand, musicologists mostly talk to each other and not to the general public. So selecting books was sometimes a somewhat subjective judgment call. Did the author write in an accessible way, or was the book clearly designed for scholars and specialists?

So I made some judgment calls. I tried not to include more than one book by a particular author. With Alan Lomax, this made for some difficult decisions, because it would be easy to regard all of the John and Alan Lomax songbooks as "must-have" items. I should also frankly say that a couple of books are on this list that I don't think are especially well done, but they cover subjects that no one else has written about. In effect, I chose the subject as an important study rather than the book itself.

There were some patterns that recurred in many of the books that I read. Folklorists and ethnomusicologists tend to print melodies without chords. For the scholar or the unaccompanied singer, this is all very well. If one of the goals of a book is to circulate the tunes that are printed, this seems to present an unnecessary barrier. Many amateur and even some fairly skilled musicians learn songs largely through finding the chords before they learn the melody. What surprised me was the number of relatively recent books that adopted this practice. In 1940 guitar players were relatively few. That is hardly true today.

In the case of instructional music, sometimes I didn't select a book in a particular category because no one book stood out to me as being significantly better or different from others. For the most part, the books covered are well researched and reasonably well written, and they discuss subjects that I feel will continue to be important and interesting fifty years from now. Most but not all of them are in print. I hope the reader will agree with my choices, but inevitably some readers may find that a favorite book doesn't appear in this volume.

THE FOLK 100

Historical Surveys

I USE THE WORD "HISTORICAL" IN A FAIRLY LOOSE WAY. THESE are not standard history texts but examinations of folk music that are written to cover a time span rather than books about a current, specific subject.

1. *Finding Her Voice: The Saga of Women in Country Music.* By Mary A. Bufwack and Robert K. Oermann. New York: Crown Publications, 1993

The title says it all. If you have any curiosity about the role of women in country music, this book is an essential guide.

There is hardly any aspect of the role of women in country music history omitted in this book. The authors begin with the role of women in mountain music. Throughout the book are photos and illustrations of dozens of female artists. In the margins of each page the authors have tables covering such details as repertoire, profiles of artists, and lists of various artists.

Early folk music presenters like Jean Thomas are covered as well as cowgirls and songs that discuss women. Among the latter are the notorious murdered-girl ballads that discuss tragic events that include marauding men and women as victims.

Every event in country music history is presented from the standpoint of how women were involved. Early performers on the Grand Ole Opry, mountain festival performers, songwriters, western performers like Patsy Montana, and radio artists like Lulu Belle and Lily May Ledford are all profiled in some depth.

Later in the book, such country songwriters as Cindy Walker, comedienne Minnie Pearl, and Kitty Wells and the way the Nashville establishment dealt with these artists are all part of this engrossing history. As the book progresses, we learn about artists with a foot in rock and roll like Wanda Jackson and Brenda Lee, women who wrote and performed music for children, and more modern mountain musicians, like Hedy West and Jean Ritchie.

No book about women in country music could omit Loretta Lynn, Patsy Cline, and Dolly Parton, and Bufwack and Oermann detail their careers. Later sections discuss women in bluegrass and pop-country artists like Barbara Mandrell and Reba McEntire. The authors are able to discuss developments like the encroachment of pop music into country in an artist like Olivia Newton-John without choosing sides.

The final section of the book includes the development of women singer-songwriters in country, the folk-influenced work of Mary Chapin Carpenter and Nanci Griffith, and country-rock artists like Lorrie Morgan and Tanya Tucker. There is an extensive bibliography keyed to each artist.

A revision of this seminal work would certainly be good news. In the meantime, it remains an essential reference.

2. *The English and Scottish Popular Ballads, Volume V.*
Edited by Francis James Child. Original edition,
1898. Mineola, NY: Dover Publications, 2003

Child's collection is the holy grail of ballads from England
and Scotland. It contains the basic classificatory system that
has defined the English ballad. Virtually every American collection also references this book because so many of these
songs have also been collected in the United States.

The collection appears in five volumes because of the
massive length of the collection. Volume V alone has over
eight hundred pages. Each ballad includes a discussion of the
ballad before Child prints the actual lyrics. These are not brief
descriptions of the songs but detailed discussions that sometimes extend to a half-dozen pages of text.

Child died before this last volume of the collection
appeared. It was shepherded by Professor George Lyman
Kittredge, who in turn was one of John Lomax's teachers and
a major influence on his own collecting of American folk
songs.

Although the book is about British and Scottish ballads,
Child's all-encompassing scholarship led him to reference
similar songs in Russian, Italian, Finnish, and Estonian versions. Child also had to wrestle with the work of Percy and
other collectors, who made their own editorial changes to the
songs.

Child's tome is an extremely scholarly work and is not
recommended for the casual fan. It includes an extensive glossary, dozens of pages of additions and corrections, but less
than fifty actual melodies for the ballads. There is an extensive bibliography, followed by a 1906 (!) essay on Child by
Walter Morris Hart. That essay is replete with class biases and
betrays the social snobbery of its author.

3. *Romancing the Folk: Public Memory & American Roots Music.* By Benjamin Filene. Chapel Hill: University of North Carolina Press, 2000

Filene has undertaken a detailed history of the sources of the folk music revival. His book covers scholarly interest in the music, the whole notion of authenticity, and the work of various key folklorists, artists, and Chess Records. It concludes with a chapter on Pete Seeger and Bob Dylan.

Filene begins with the British folklorists, explaining how Thomas Percy admitted making additions and corrections to traditional songs. He then moves on to English folk music in the United States and the role of the settlement schools in preserving the music and in offering a base for British musicologist Cecil Sharp to collect music in the southern mountains. He sees Sharp as someone who retained a sort of upper-class snobbishness but at the same time sincerely wanted to revive the songs that he collected, not simply archive them. He also points out that Sharp had no interest in collecting songs by African Americans.

John Lomax, southern redneck warts and all, whatever his plantation-era shortcomings, understood that African American music was "the most distinctive—the most interesting, the most appealing, and the greatest in quantity." This statement, made in 1934, in Lomax's *American Ballads and Folksongs*, is astounding, considering that at that time there were still many folklorists whose primary collecting interest was in finding American survivals of British traditional ballads.

The chapter on Leadbelly and the Lomaxes shows how Leadbelly was presented as a sort of exotic animal, fascinating to observe but not entirely to be trusted. Both John and Alan Lomax were concerned the northern audiences would not be able to understand Leadbelly's dialect, and they "may" have encouraged him to insert extended spoken dialogues in his songs. Since this became a key part of Leadbelly's performances, the question of whether it was the Lomaxes who suggested this is an important and unresolved one.

By 1941 the work of the Lomaxes, with Alan taking a more active role in their "partnership," treated the music more as a living thing than an antique museum piece. This also was influenced by the work of Charles Seeger and the amount of folk song collecting that was part of various federal programs in the 1930s.

The material on Chess Records and Muddy Waters is acceptable but is covered in more detail and with more insight in the several books that discuss Waters, Willie Dixon, and Chess Records.

Arguments about authenticity became significant in the study of folklore, where Richard Dorson, who established the folklore program at the University of Indiana, created the word "fakelore" to describe what he considered to be bowdlerization of pure folk songs. He did not regard published folk songs as a primary source of research, and he despised political protest songs as a distortion of the folk song tradition.

Filene concludes with a chapter that compares the work of Pete Seeger and Bob Dylan. In the author's eyes, Seeger's life has been "a work of performance art that fused his personal and professional identities into a role that he performed day and night for his entire life." Filene cuts Dylan considerably more slack, seeing his later work as an extension of the folk tradition. His final statement on Dylan is that "even in a postindustrial, pop rock culture, a folk stylist could create relevant, contemporary songs rooted in tradition."

Filene's book is important because it leads us to investigate folk music in terms of its role as a living art versus the attempt to create a sort of alternate universe by people longing for some nonmodern, utopian world. Sometimes Filene overreaches; for example, Dylan's persona is easily as artificially constructed (or more so) as that of Pete Seeger. And

Seeger himself has written an interesting body of instrumental music and some major songs, which, like Dylan's, continue to have a life of their own far beyond his own performances. Referring to Samuel Charters as a major blues collector for two decades is a bit misleading. Charters did not collect a body of songs and did not, like Harry Oster, Alan Lomax, Ed Denson, and various other people discover or rediscover Skip James, John Hurt, Son House, and Mance Lipscomb. What he did do was to record or to reissue important blues recordings and to write in an accessible, somewhat romanticized style that brought many fans and musicians into the blues revival.

4. *Country Music USA*. By Bill C. Malone. Revised edition. Austin: University of Texas Press, 1997

Beginning with the folk roots of country music, this book offers a thorough and well-balanced history of country music.

Malone offers extensive coverage of virtually every conceivable idiom of country music. Most readers will find the coverage quite complete, at least up until the date of its publication. For those who wish to go even deeper, the author provides an unusual "bibliographical essay," ninety pages of suggested readings of books and periodicals about all of the specific styles represented in the book.

The role of western music is well documented, from the radio cowboys of the 1930s, through the development of Texas swing, to the more modern cowboy revivalist bands like Riders in the Sky. Since this area of the country music story is often minimized or neglected, this coverage is welcome. Other sections of the book document early "hillbilly music," various incarnations of pop-country music, Elvis and rock and roll's relationship to country music, bluegrass, and the outlaws' rebellion against the Nashville establishment.

There is very little missing in this comprehensive portrait of the history and development of country music. Possibly

Malone might have offered more coverage of the Nashville studios and the musicians who are largely responsible for the development of the Nashville sound. Many of the changes in that sound came from the replacement of the first generation of Nashville studio players by a more rebellious and musically diverse set of musicians. It was largely the presence of such musicians as Kenny Buttrey, Norbert Putnam, and Charlie McCoy that brought many of the folk and rock musicians to Music City to record. The resulting recordings in turn influenced more traditional country music to expand its horizons.

This is a small flaw in an excellently researched and well-documented book. This is the sort of work that will infiltrate your consciousness, lead you to read other books about specific country music styles, and induce you to listen to much music that you have not heard before.

5. *Bluegrass: A History.* By Neil V. Rosenberg. Twentieth anniversary edition. Urbana: University of Illinois Press, 2005

Rosenberg is a bluegrass musician, folklorist, and college professor. This book is a comprehensive history of bluegrass music through 1974, with a short chapter through the mid-1980s and a brief preface covering the music through the early 2000s.

There are surprisingly few histories of bluegrass music available, given the presence of numerous summer and winter festivals, recordings, and the emergence of Alison Krauss and the movie soundtracks that have featured the music. Rosenberg is, for the most part, a reliable and fair-minded guide.

The book begins with the musical history of Bill Monroe. The author is careful to avoid some of the controversies that have emerged with the music. Monroe is generally regarded as the father and possibly the single most important originator of the music. However, his own music crystallized when Lester Flatt and Earl Scruggs joined the band in 1945. Scruggs's banjo style was certainly very influential in the development of bluegrass, but in 1948 Flatt and Scruggs left Monroe and formed their own band, Lester Flatt and Earl Scruggs and the Foggy Mountain Boys.

Louise Scruggs, Earl's wife, handled the business of the new group, and she was able to secure endorsement deals with Martha White Flour. The author details Scruggs's successful recordings, including "Foggy Mountain Breakdown," used in the movie *Bonnie and Clyde*, and "The Ballad of Jed Clampett," which was the theme from the TV show *The Beverly Hillbillies*. Meanwhile, various musicians passed through Monroe's band, which other than some brief guidance from Ralph Rinzler lacked any sort of managerial expertise.

The author also details the emergence of "newgrass" music, using a more jazz-oriented and technical musical approach. He also shows how some of the newgrass musicians irritated traditionalists by growing "hippie" hairstyles and being involved in the 1960s drug scene. Eventually the level of musicianship of some of the newgrass players, like Bela Fleck and Sam Bush, gained the grudging respect of traditionalists, if not their allegiance.

We also learn how Monroe himself, though always in the traditionalist camp, began to hire musicians from the North and other parts of the country to join his band. Bill ("Brad") Keith from Boston caused quite a stir with his melodic banjo playing, Richard Greene brought his fiddle playing from northern California, and other musicians were welcomed, even from the dreaded Yankee enclave of New York City. Rosenberg fully appreciates the irony of Monroe bringing these non-Appalachian musicians into the fold while at the same time maintaining his role as the father of traditional bluegrass music.

In addition to discussing the music itself, the author covers the business of bluegrass, the emergence of the various specialty record companies that marketed the music, and the organizations, festivals, and periodicals that contributed to the music. This has turned bluegrass into a definite niche in the world of country and folk music.

If you are seeking a reliable guide to the history of the music, this book should meet your needs.

The omission of Bobby Thompson, the banjoist who developed melodic banjo techniques at about the same time as Bill Keith did and who was a staff musician on the *Hee Haw* show and played on dozens of country and bluegrass recordings, is a bit puzzling. The skimpy introductory chapter does not really bring the reader up to date, and the book is really in need of revision to cover bluegrass music today. The extensive discography unfortunately will prove worthless to most readers because it ends with the LP era, and it doesn't include any CDs.

6. *The Beautiful Music All Around Us: Field Recordings and the American Experience.* By Stephen Wade. Urbana: University of Illinois Press, 2012

Wade is a musician and recording artist who has written and performed several shows based on American roots music. In this book, Wade profiles a dozen performers who recorded for the Library of Congress between 1934 and 1942. In putting together the stories of each performer, he researched them, their families, and their peers as best he could, and he re-created the ambiance of the actual performances as accurately as possible. An accompanying CD includes tracks from each of the artists.

None of these artists became nationally known celebrities, but Vera Hall, Pete Steele, and Texas Gladden are well known to folklorists and serious fans of traditional music.

With the exception of Pete Steele, who recorded in Hamilton, Ohio, the artists were recorded in various southern states.

One of the joys that comes with reading this book is an understanding of how a song that we are used to hearing in a specific way has a rich history of its own. For example, on the CD is a song called "The Rock Island Line," sung by Kelly Pace and a group of prisoners in Arkansas.

Many of our readers will be familiar with Leadbelly's version of this song, which was also a hit record for English skiffle artist Lonnie Donnegan. The recorded version is similar to the one that Leadbelly popularized. The book prints what was the original version of the song, which was composed by singer and engine wiper Clarence Wilson. That version of the song includes a chorus similar to the more celebrated version, but the verses mention specific people, like the engineer, who did not survive in Leadbelly's rendition or in the one recorded here. Wade then goes on to discuss the railroad itself and the Biddle Shops Colored Quartet, which the company sponsored.

There are far too many such nuggets in the book to be reproduced here. We read about John Work III recording the Nashville Washboard Band as his son John Work IV recalls the event. "These people," he recalls, "*were* their music." The group played on the streets of Nashville, performing on guitar, washboard, banjo-mandolin, and bass. Two of the men were blind, and three of them were day laborers.

Pete Steele, the one person recorded outside the South, was formerly a Kentucky coal miner who moved to Ohio after he became afflicted with black lung disease. His 1938 Library of Congress recording of the "Coal Creek March" went on to become a sort of testing ground for urban banjo players some twenty-five years later. Wade describes the history of the Coal Creek mine disasters, and he also offers details about how Steele learned these pieces and about other musicians' renditions of them.

This is a wonderful book, and the recording is the whipped cream on top of the cake, giving us an aural window into Wade's informative and passionate words.

Biographies and Autobiographies

These books are presented in alphabetical order by the name of the subject, not the author.

7. *DeFord Bailey: A Black Star in Early Country Music.* By David C. Morton with Charles K. Wolfe. Knoxville: University of Tennessee Press, 1991

DeFord Bailey was the first (and for years the only) African American performer on the Grand Ole Opry. After he left the Opry, little was known about Bailey's life. Morton encountered him in his capacity as an employee of the public housing authority in Nashville. Morton made contact with Bailey while working on a newsletter for the housing authority and became interested in learning about Bailey's life and career. This book is the fortunate result of that quest.

As with so many black musicians of the early twentieth century, Bailey's life involved overcoming childhood tragedy. DeFord Bailey was born in 1899. Two tragic events quickly marred his childhood. His mother died when Bailey was only a year old, and Bailey was basically adopted by his father's youngest sister. At the age of three, Bailey developed a case of polio. He did recover from the disease, but his growth was stunted and he was left with a slightly deformed back.

The Bailey family was very musical, and at family gatherings and local dances played what Bailey himself called "black hillbilly music." Various members of the family played harmonica, fiddle, guitar, and banjo, and many also sang. As Morton and his coauthor Charles Wolfe tell the story, Bailey's career on the Opry was an accidental event. An Opry cast member named Dr. Humphrey Bate invited Bailey to play with him on WSM. This took some convincing because Bailey had a cheap harmonica and felt embarrassed to share the stage with a bunch of fancy guitars and banjos. And, of course, all the other musicians were white.

Bailey's harmonica playing created such a stir that soon he was appearing regularly on the Opry. He also made some records for the Brunswick Company, including train and animal imitations among them. The records sold well enough that Bailey began to resent the excessive commissions that the Opry took on his work and his low salary for playing on the radio. He made a foray into Knoxville, where he proved to be quite successful. Becoming restless, he was tempted to try California, but after he decided against that move he returned to Nashville, where he worked on the Opry, and also started to go out on personal appearance tours.

The tours were difficult for Bailey because he was the only black artist in the group. Some restaurants wouldn't feed him, so he took to eating in the kitchen, as though he were a cook. Banjo picker and Opry star Uncle Dave Macon treated him with respect and would sneak him into his hotel room under the pretense that Bailey was his valet. The book's stories about white and black interactions are fascinating. Bailey had a boarding house and got into trouble with the Ku Klux Klan because he was renting rooms to both white and black renters. Klan members even burned a cross in his backyard to make their point.

In May 1941, Bailey was fired from the Opry. As Morton and Wolfe explain the story, part of it had to do with the controversies between the two major performing rights organizations who license songs for radio play. The Opry supported the newcomer, BMI, and asked its artists not to play ASCAP tunes. The station engaged in a boycott of ASCAP tunes and requested that Bailey learn new, BMI-controlled songs. This was difficult for him because he was an improvising stylist who did not write songs but created his own arrangements of them. The songs that he was performing were older, ASCAP songs. This led to Bailey's dismissal.

DeFord Bailey then opened a shoe-shine stand and curtailed his music career. During the 1960s Bailey's son DeFord Jr. played saxophone on a soul radio show, and his father joined him from time to time. He also did some shows for the Washington Folklore Society. Bailey also played on some Opry reunion shows and turned down a chance to play three songs for $2,500 in the movie *W.W. and the Dixie Dancekings.*

Bailey had become somewhat bitter because he realized that he had been taken advantage of during the Grand Ole Opry years. It is a tribute to David Morton that he was able to gain Bailey's confidence to the point where he shared so much of his life story. Although the book is mostly biographical, there are some descriptions of Bailey's harmonica technique. It is a shame that no CD was included with this book. The chances are that virtually none of the readers of this book have ever heard DeFord Bailey play the harmonica.

8. *I Feel So Good: The Life and Times of Big Bill Broonzy.* By Bob Riesman. Chicago: University of Chicago Press, 2011

There have been a number of significant figures in the history of Chicago blues who were important not only because of their own music but because they acted as mentors, friends, and informal business agents for other blues artists. Tampa Red, Big Bill Broonzy, and Muddy Waters come to mind as the most influential of these musicians. Riesman's book is a detailed discussion of not only Broonzy's life but the various legends, often promoted by the artist himself, that grew up around the life and career of Big Bill Broonzy.

One of the reasons this is an important book is that many folklorists and folk song collectors seem to assume that their informants are basically truthful and err on factual details only because of the passing of time. Broonzy, on the other hand, was an inveterate storyteller, whose "facts" are a function of what he is trying to describe. For example, there is the matter of Bill's name. His real name was "probably" Lee Conley Bradley.

When you consider that the artist has changed his own name, it doesn't come as much of a surprise when the author uncovers contradictory stories about when Broonzy learned to read and write, whether his uncle Jerry Belcher actually existed, and on and on. Riesman shows how Broonzy could be a musical chameleon, combining different musical styles, and, like Lightnin' Hopkins and Muddy Waters, alternating between roles as a country acoustic bluesman and a sort of pre–rhythm and blues combo artist. Riesman shows that for all Broonzy's ability to adapt to change and roll with the punches, like many other artists he was victimized by the music industry, giving up 75 percent of his publishing and songwriting royalties as opposed to the more typical 50 percent. Basically, what this means is that Broonzy gave up not only publishing rights, which is not especially unusual even today, but also half of his songwriting royalties.

Another interesting portion of the book describes the segregated history of the musicians' union. The black local of the union in Chicago had nine hundred members in 1939, and as the author tells the story, many were attracted to the death insurance benefit that the local paid to the families of deceased members.

Broonzy mastered the electric guitar well enough to accompany Lil Green in the 1940s. Later in the decade Bill helped a young Muddy Waters become established on the Chicago club scene. Other Chicago blues musicians, like Jimmy Rogers and Little Walter, also credited Bill for helping them become established. Other parts of the book describe

Bill's successful European tours and his career in the folk revival.

The final word on Bill's elaborations or revisions of facts is the author's comment, "He began with something that actually did happen, and then created a tale that conveyed the key elements of the story in ways he believed would hold the attention of the listener." Riesman has come as far as anyone I can imagine in untangling the facts from the hyperbole.

9. *Natalie Curtis Burlin: A Life in Native and African American Music.* By Michelle Wick Patterson. Lincoln: University of Nebraska Press, 2010

This is a biography of Natalie Curtis Burlin. Burlin was a classically trained concert pianist from a wealthy New York family. Like a number of her contemporaries, like Dorothy Scarborough, Frances Densmore, and Alice Fletcher, she became fascinated by "primitive" music.

The significance of this book is that it pays tribute to a collector of folk songs who is a woman. Most of the existing discussions of folk music scholars focus on the omnipresent Lomax family and on other males, such as Carl Sandburg. Although Burlin was a trained musician, she was self-trained as an ethnomusicologist and anthropologist. Her two-hundred-page collection of the music of American Indians, *The Indians' Book*, was published in 1907 and remains in print today.

As part of her quest to collect and transcribe American Indian music, Burlin studied African American music at the Hampton Institute. This led to her later writing books about African American and African music.

Interaction with Hopi and Navajo people transformed Burlin from a somewhat patronizing dabbler into a scholar with a deep appreciation for the music and culture of her informants. Patterson points out that Burlin credited her sources, naming singers and others who contributed drawings to her books. Unlike those of more formally trained ethnomusicologists, like Densmore, Burlin's books were intended for a wide audience. Burlin also lobbied for improvement of the living conditions of American Indians while her peers either maintained their scientific objectivity or even encouraged reservation dwellers to sell off their land.

In working with African American music, Burlin used grant money to promote concerts, and in her studies of the music she attempted to connect the music to its African origins. As she had done with American Indians, Burlin supported reforms designed to benefit African Americans. She fought to desegregate the armed forces in World War I, and after moving to Paris with her husband she defended the music that she had collected against the patronizing attitudes of a Harvard professor at a music conference. This amazingly energetic woman also composed three songs based on traditional Mexican American pieces.

This is one of the best balanced biographies that I have read. The author frankly describes Burlin's romantic and occasionally patronizing attitudes toward her informants. When we consider that she died in 1921, the amazing scope of her interests and publications makes an excellent book worthy of your attention.

10. *Will You Miss Me When I'm Gone? The Carter Family & Their Legacy in American Music.* By Mark Zwonitzer with Charles Hirshberg. New York: Simon and Schuster, 2002

The Carter Family was one of the most influential artists in the history of country music, and over time this influence filtered into the folk music revival. This is a biography of the family, A. P.; his wife, Sara; and Sara's cousin Maybelle, who married A. P.'s father.

The cast of characters discussed includes a number of other family members, including the family's daughters, June, Helen, and Anita, as well as June's (eventual) husband, Johnny Cash. There are also many details of the family's life in the Clinch Mountain area of Virginia and of how the family moved from living in abject poverty to being recording, radio, and performing artists.

One of the most fascinating portions of the book is A. P.'s friendship with African American guitarist Lesley Riddle. Riddle had a superb musical memory, and A. P. and Lesley traveled together through the mountains. A. P. would persuade an informant to sing, and Lesley would then act as a human tape recorder, remembering both the tune and the lyrics. The family would then learn and record the songs. A. P. and Lesley's friendship and traveling together was a bit unusual for the time, and sometimes A. P. would have to scramble to come up with places where Lesley was welcome to stay.

There are also interesting details about the influence of Ralph Peer in the recording industry. Peer had a deal with RCA Records where he produced recordings for no fee but got to own the music publishing rights of the songs. As part of this discussion, the authors describe how the Carters sometimes wrote original songs but also often cobbled together songs from lyric or melodic fragments that they collected in the mountains. In other instances they revised or edited old poems and broadsides. When A. P. and Sara divorced, the family continued to record and write despite Sara's move to California.

Johnny Cash's addition to the family provided a new source of jobs and recording work for Maybelle, who was also rediscovered and newly appreciated for her guitar and autoharp artistry during the folk music revival. The Nitty Gritty Dirt Band's multi-album set, *Will the Circle Be Unbroken?*, featured Maybelle on a number of cuts.

This is an absorbing story about the "first family" of country music. Once a seemingly endless description of family history is detailed during the early part of the book, it makes for fascinating reading. It is unfortunate that the authors did not choose to include any sort of discography of the family's recordings.

11. *"I'd Give My Life": From Washington Square to Carnegie Hall; A Journey by Folk Music.* By Erik Darling. Palo Alto, CA: Science and Behavior Books, 2008

This is an autobiography from the founding member of the Tarriers and the Rooftop Singers.

Although he is not well known to the general public, Darling was a universally respected figure in the folk music community. This book is a heartfelt, emotional description of his life in and out of music. One of the most affecting parts of the book is his reminiscences of Nicky Thatcher, a little-known blues singer and heroin addict whom Darling knew in the 1950s. In doubt as to his musical identity, Darling wonders whether a musician needs to abuse himself in order to attain an original style.

There is a very funny chapter called "The Folksinger Who Came to Dinner." Darling shuttled back and forth between his father, who was a painter living in upstate New York, and his mother, who had an apartment on West Sixty-Eighth Street in New York City. Folksinger and brilliant instrumentalist Frank Hamilton came to dinner and ended up staying for weeks, finally leaving after some conflicts with Darling's mother.

Gradually Darling's musical career became more viable. First the Tarriers had a hit record with the calypso-flavored tune "Day-O." They suffered the usual record-company injustices, and then Darling left the group and became Pete Seeger's replacement in the Weavers.

Erik Darling was a free-thinking individual whose views were generally libertarian. Suddenly he was thrust into a group whose political views were basically tied in with politics close to or in the middle of the ideology of the Communist Party. Mutual musical respect seemed to bridge that gap. The group traveled to Europe, and Erik brought his new wife, Joan. There is a very funny story about Lee Hays and an overflowing bathtub, which readers can discover for themselves.

By 1962 Erik left the Weavers and formed the Rooftop Singers with Bill Svanoe, Lynn Taylor, and (initially) his old friend Tommy Geraci. The book tells the painful story of how Geraci was fired from the group, also damaging a long-term friendship. The group then went on to have a huge hit with the song "Walk Right In." Eventually that group fell apart, and Erik went on to become a counselor, living variously in Vail, near Santa Fe, and toward the end of his life in North Carolina. In his final years there was a Weavers reunion concert, a video, and several other recordings. Erik died in 2008, just as this book was coming out.

Erik Darling deserves much more credit than has been given to him in the various books about the folk song revival. Whether as an accompanist for Ed McCurdy and others or as a vocal and instrumental arranger with several hit groups, his music will survive and be revived over the years. In this book, his observations about the relationships between men and women are thoughtful and sensitive. They reveal a person with the capacity for love but who never quite succeeded in formulating a single long-term relationship. His insights into his own habits and behavior make for an interesting contrast with the egomaniacal biographies and autobiographies of many of the other figures in the folk music revival.

The accompanying CD contains a few of Erik's major works, including "Train Time" and "Walk Right In." If you're not familiar with Erik or his music or you simply want to know more about him, be sure to find this book.

12. *Truth Is Stranger Than Fiction.* By Alton Delmore. Edited by Charles K. Wolfe. Nashville: Country Music Foundation Press, 1995

The Delmore Brothers were one of a number of groups that had one foot firmly in the world of country music and the other in folk music. When John Lomax and other folk song scholars were doing their fieldwork in the 1920s and 1930s, they tended to dismiss professional musicians who recorded, performed on the radio, and toured. The prevailing folkloristic attitude was that professional musicians were contaminated by the world of pop and had lost the pristine qualities that folklorists attributed to "rural" folksingers.

Because of the prevalence of these attitudes, folk fans and future generations never really learned about the lives and repertoires of such performers as the Blue Sky Boys, the Shelton Brothers, Uncle Dave Macon, and many others. By the 1950s Alan Lomax and others realized that many of the so-called commercial country performers had a large repertoire that included folk songs as well as original songs that were substantially influenced by earlier musical styles.

Subsequently, recent studies of younger musicians like Doc Watson have enabled us to gain some insights into this rich body of music.

The story of this particular book is that Alton Delmore had worked on it for some years but had given up on getting it published. After his death, folk scholar Charles Wolfe discovered the manuscript with the help of Lionel Delmore, a successful Nashville songwriter and Alton's son. The initial full copy of the manuscript was missing, but various friends and relatives were able to fill in some of the missing chapters with their own copies.

The Delmores were born in north Alabama. Alton, the older brother, was born in 1908 and Rabon in 1916. Their childhood, like that of many country and blues performers, is depicted here as one of almost constant, grinding poverty. They performed together from 1926 to 1952. By the time Alton was in ninth grade, he was singing, mostly gospel songs. One of the things Alton reveals is that unlike most country musicians of his day, he could read and write music and had a basic knowledge of music theory. As Rabon grew older, the brothers began to play at fiddlers' gatherings, and Alton wrote the song "Brown's Ferry Blues," which is still performed by country and folk musicians today. Alton provides a view of the Grand Ole Opry that is both enlightening and depressing. Although the Delmores were the most popular act on the show in 1936 and sold more records than any other acts on the show, they were continually humiliated and exploited by Opry management. The book chronicles the endless drives through the southern countryside to make it back for the show on Saturday.

Delmore goes on to describe a successful audition for Columbia Records, followed by a similar success at WSM, home of the Grand Ole Opry. Alton describes how the audition succeeded despite the brothers missing the initial time set for it. The Opry paid poorly, and so the acts on the show were obligated to tour constantly. As they exhausted their appeal in a specific geographic area, they had to travel farther away, making the Saturday night shows pure torture. So the brothers traveled in beat-up cars on bad roads, in rain and sunshine, and learned how to protect themselves from various sharks in the industry, in and out of the Opry, who wanted to appropriate their songs without credit. A recommendation from a fellow musician resulted in an attempt to recruit the boys for radio station WLS in Chicago. The Opry overlords then exaggerated and even lied to the Delmores about matching opportunities offered by the Chicago station. After an initial wage increase, their wages were cut back, and consequently, they were compelled to increase the number of their personal appearances. And, of course, the WLS opportunity vanished.

One of the great values of this book is Alton's candid and self-effacing observations about the industry and his fellow performers. Because the brothers traveled with Opry fixtures like Uncle Dave Macon and DeFord Bailey, the book has many anecdotes of what it was like to perform during the 1930s and 1940s. Alton describes in detail the best guitar player he ever saw, a man who asked to borrow Alton's guitar after a radio show in Memphis. The stranger was poorly dressed, and after he played some spectacular guitar for the brothers, they gave him ten dollars and asked him to come back. They never saw him again.

Eventually the brothers went on to record for King Records in Cincinnati and move to various other radio stations, and they got to play in some theater chains in the southern states. In 1952 Rabon contracted lung cancer and died that August. Alton survived for another twelve years by teaching guitar and from his songwriting royalties. This book provides a realistic picture of what it was like to be a country-folk musician playing on the Grand Ole Opry, touring small towns all over the South, and always struggling to make a living. It is the most realistic portrait of this life that I have encountered.

13. *Working Girl Blues: The Life & Music of Hazel Dickens.* By Hazel Dickens and Bill C. Malone. Urbana: University of Illinois Press, 2008

Hazel Dickens is not a household name in country music. This book is her story, a combination biography and songbook, including forty of her songs.

Born and raised in a West Virginia coal-mining community, Dickens moved to Baltimore at the age of sixteen. She settled in a section of the city filled with hillbilly expatriates like herself. Malone describes how she became friendly with a social worker and fiddler named Alyse Taubman. who encouraged her to play the music she had learned in her family. Through her brother, Dickens met a young Mike Seeger, already an accomplished instrumentalist, who was working in a tuberculosis sanatorium. Seeger began to play music with Alyse and two of her brothers. Dickens then began to work part-time in clubs with a band that included Mike Seeger on fiddle.

Experiencing a certain amount of male chauvinist discrimination in the clubs made Hazel focus on songs that related to her own life and experiences. Dickens then met city-raised Alice Foster, and they formed a duo. After an early local performance, they did an album for Folkways in 1965, which led to another album several years later.

As Malone tells it, a three-year marriage and a divorce led Dickens to move to Washington, DC, in 1969. She managed a retail store weekdays and did music at night and on weekends. It was during this period that Dickens wrote a number of songs that described the life of coal miners. Malone goes on to describe Dickens's career. She sang in a band called the Strange Creek Singers, with Foster and Mike Seeger. They played folk festivals, and Hazel and Alice went on to record for Rounder Records. In 1986 she sang her songs for the movie *Matewan*, which brought her to the attention of many new fans.

The balance of the book, after a half-dozen photos, consists of the lyrics of Dickens's songs, along with her explanations of why the songs were written. Some of the songs describe her own life situation, like "Don't Put Her Down, You

Helped Put Her There," and others are about social issues or simply her own observations about life.

Hazel Dickens died in 2011, but thanks to Bill Malone we have access to her songs and the story of her life. It is unfortunate that the book does not include the music to any of her songs.

14. *I Am the Blues: The Willie Dixon Story.* By Willie Dixon with Don Snowden. New York: Da Capo, 1989

This is an "as told to" autobiography, which relates the long and fascinating life of a Chicago blues songwriter, bassist, record producer, and music publisher. Dixon was a key component in the Chess Records sound. He worked closely with Muddy Waters, Howlin' Wolf, Chuck Berry, and numerous other artists.

Willie wore so many hats that it is difficult to attribute his importance to a particular skill. In a world dominated by white business executives, he carved out a role for himself as a record producer and music arranger who was the key figure in many of the records that he worked on. As a person working in virtually every aspect of the business and art of blues in Chicago, he is uniquely qualified to tell the story of how the Mississippi blues were transformed into early rhythm and blues.

One of the major aspects of the book is the somewhat complex relationship that existed between Chess Records, owned by two Jewish brothers from Chicago, and the black artists whose music the brothers merchandised. Dixon relates how his publishing was owned by a company called Arc Music, whose ownership was split between the Chess brothers and two of Benny Goodman's brothers who worked out of New York City.

The Chess brothers, as Dixon tells the story, did care about their artists and the music, but they also tended to have a patriarchal relationship with the artists, and even with Dixon. This seems especially odd to this writer, given that Dixon's songs were the vehicle to put over most of the artists that he worked with. Without these songs, in effect, Chess had nothing to sell. Eventually, Dixon sued to get back the rights to his songs. Along the way, he also had to sue Led Zeppelin, who transformed Dixon's song "You Need Love" into their song "Whole Lotta Love."

Although Dixon was generally liked and respected by his peers, there are also those who claim that he placed his name on songs that he did not write or that were not so much compositions as elaborations of earlier songs. Some of these details are chronicled in another work, more detailed but less readable, *Willie Dixon: Preacher of the Blues*, by Mitsutoshi Inaba.

15. *Bob Dylan Chronicles, Volume 1*. By Bob Dylan. New York: Simon and Schuster, 2004

There are so many books, videos, and documentaries that have been written about Bob Dylan that one almost gets the feeling that this autobiographical work was written in self-defense!

Almost all the biographies of Dylan seem to resolve into the authors' frustrations about exactly who Bob Dylan is. Is he a protest singer, a surrealist, a greedy capitalist who simply tailors his music to trends, a seriously religious prophet leading us out of the wilderness, a musical genius, or simply a self-centered narcissist?

As *Chronicles* evolves, the reader senses that Dylan is possibly all of these things. The reader's predilections toward Dylan and his work will probably color his or her decisions about which of these traits is the most significant.

What stands out in this volume to me is how uncontroversial it is. In his New York days, at least, Dylan was notorious for his sarcastic put-downs. The reader won't find much of this here. Karen Dalton was his favorite singer in Greenwich Village. Dave Van Ronk was a real mentor in New York. John Hammond was a good friend who understood Dylan. Numerous other friends and associates let him stay at their apartments, read their books, or listen to their records. Who would ever have thought that Dylan would write a book that is virtually "all good?"

The other aspect of this book that stands out is Dylan's time travel. The book simply does not appear to have been edited. We time travel from the 1960s to the 1980s or from the 1990s to the 1970s without any discernible reason.

There are many redeeming aspects to this book. It is an excellent description of the Greenwich Village folk world circa 1960. The casual nature of the lifestyles, the quickly formed and easily dissipated friendships, and the musicians struggling to survive but not needing much money to get from one day to the next. Another surprise in the book is that Dylan rarely refers to money in any way. For a person generally regarded as being extremely ambitious, this is a bit of a surprise.

Dylan's stories about his encounters with the poet Archibald MacLeish, who wanted Dylan to collaborate on music for a play, are wonderful. They reveal a more respectful and introspective person than many readers would expect to find. Similarly, his stories of recording with Daniel Lanois and Bob Johnston reveal some of his ambitions and frustrations.

It is interesting that Dylan has titled the book *Volume 1*. One assumes that the saga will continue in future volumes. Or, given Dylan's mysterious persona, maybe not.

16. *African American Folksong and American Cultural Politics: The Lawrence Gellert Story.* By Bruce M. Conforth. Lanham, MD: Scarecrow Press, 2013

Lawrence Gellert is one of the most mysterious figures in the entire history of the folk song revival in the United States.

Conforth's biography of Gellert attempts to evaluate Gellert's legacy in the pantheon of folk song collectors, and to reveal the many peculiar details of his life.

Gellert was born into a radical Hungarian American émigré family. Hugo Gellert, one of his brothers, was an artist and an editor for the essentially Communist journal the *New Masses*, while brother Ernest was a conscientious objector in World War I who was murdered while imprisoned in an army camp. In an attempt to understand the many mysterious aspects of Lawrence's character, the author traces Lawrence's situation as the neglected younger brother who always seemed subservient to art star Hugo and to his two other brothers. Both of them became successful business men.

Gellert's contribution to folk music was that he lived on and off in North Carolina during the early 1920s and into the 1930s and collected music from many African American informants.

During the 1930s, he compiled two folios of protest songs, which are basically what established his reputation as a unique music collector. Conforth shows that these songs were greatly exceeded by more standard folk song offerings that Gellert found in his travels, along with a sizable number of folk tales.

Gellert's brother Hugo encouraged him to collect and publish protest songs for inclusion in Communist and Communist-leaning publications, as did Nancy Cunard, one of his many female partners. Conforth even cites some evidence indicating that Gellert himself was relatively apolitical, at least compared to brother Hugo.

Gellert became involved with controversies with the Lomaxes over their treatment of Leadbelly and also because of his resentment at their ignoring his work in their own collections. More controversy erupted when Josh White recorded a half-dozen songs that Gellert collected without crediting him as the source of the songs. The reader should be aware that it was customary at the time for folk song collectors to copyright songs either in their name or as coauthors of the songs. In any case, Gellert's complaints to John Hammond at Columbia Records apparently produced some sort of financial settlement for him.

Part of Conforth's thesis is that Gellert at the very least solicited his informants to write songs of protest or complaint and that quite possibly he edited some of their lyrics to emphasize these aspects of the songs. This is quite plausible, though not entirely unique. For example, there was John Lomax's fruitless attempt to get Blind Willie McTell to sing such songs, and one might ask whether Leadbelly would ever have written his song "Bourgeois Blues" without the encouragement of Alan Lomax. The author has researched whatever Gellert material is available and has concluded that protest music represents only a small percentage of Gellert's collecting work. The latter included considerable folklore as well as folk songs.

Part of the problem in evaluating Gellert's own contributions to the songs is that he kept no field notes and did not keep track of the artists whose songs he recorded. This in turn caused him problems with orthodox folklorists, to whom these were unacceptable methods.

This is a fascinating book. Although it does not entirely solve the riddle of Gellert's life and activities, it is probably as close as we will ever get to doing so. Conforth tends to minimize the protest aspect of Gellert's collections, but sometimes I get the sense that this is more of a semantic problem than anything else. What is a protest song? Must it be written by someone involved in an actual social struggle? Is a song of complaint that does not call for social change a protest song, or must a song call for change to fit this category?

Conforth outlines a number of cases where Gellert fought to keep all the rights to the songs he collected. However, in 1964 the Journeymen, the band that I was in at the time, recorded the song "Two Hobos." I split the composition rights with Gellert. This was accomplished through a music publisher named Al Brackman at Ludlow Music. There was no extended negotiation or complaint. Unfortunately, I am unable to detail any negotiation because I was not involved in it. The same song, by the way, was later recorded by Judy Roderick on her album *Woman Blue* with the same writing credits.

17. *Woody Guthrie: A Life.* By Joe Klein. New York: Random House, 1999 edition

There have been many biographies of Woody Guthrie, but this is the most fair-minded and comprehensive treatment of his life.

Currently there is a great vogue for Woody Guthrie. All sorts of folk-rock and folk artists are writing tunes for long-discarded lyrics, and a variety of biographical works, mostly tributes to his work or his politics, have appeared. What distinguishes Klein's book is his no-holds-barred treatment of Guthrie's disastrous personal life.

Born to a middle-class family in Oklahoma, Woody experienced the many ups and downs of his wheeler-dealer father's real-estate and political career. Unfortunately, Woody inherited the gene for Huntington's chorea, a debilitating disease that runs in families. As he grew up, he experienced a series of fires, something that was to haunt him throughout his life. Klein describes how Woody's sister Clara burned herself to death as a result of a foolish argument with her mother. Later, his mother threatened her husband and her condition deteriorated, so she was consigned to a mental institution.

As Klein relates the tale, Woody's musical genes came from his various relatives, especially his fiddling uncle Jeff. Trips to imaginary silver mines and all sorts of jaunts, together with his family's disorderly life, instilled the runaway spirit in Woody. Traveling to Los Angeles, he met singer Maxine "Lefty Lou" Crissman and had a successful radio duo with her in the 1930s. Eventually, Woody's adherence to party-line ideology cost him that job. Although the station owner, J. Frank Bourke, was himself a radical, he was not a party-line follower.

The author gives us insight into Woody's wayward behavior. His irresponsibility and constant need to travel destroyed his first marriage. Traveling to New York, Woody hooked up with Pete Seeger, Alan Lomax, and the Almanac Singers. Self-centered, competitive, and egotistical, Woody nonetheless was a productive lyricist and successfully passed himself off as a sort of proletarian Walt Whitman. Falling in love with and marrying dancer Marjorie Mazia, Woody replicated his previous marital pattern. He traveled constantly, was offered relatively lucrative work on radio and television, alienated the sources of his work, and traveled back to Los Angeles. Woody fathered four children with Marjorie Mazia, one of whom died in yet another fire.

Klein describes how Jack Elliott became Woody's shadow and imitator. Jack in turn tutored Arlo Guthrie and Bob Dylan, in effect teaching them how to become Woody Guthrie. Guthrie married again and fathered yet another child, this one given up for adoption.

There are no real heroes in this sad story. At his best, as the author tells it, Woody was creative and productive, and he apparently charmed many women. At his worst, he was in desperate need of an editor, mistreated rafts of women, and suffered from his disease, his childhood memories, and the death of his daughter Cathy in yet another fire.

This is a fascinating and realistic book. It offers a truthful evaluation of an enigmatic character whose legacy is currently being distorted by those who value his politics and attitude more than they comprehend the strength and limitations of his artistry and personality.

18. *Black Pearls: Blues Queens of the 1920s.* By Daphne Duval Harrison. New Brunswick, NJ: Rutgers University Press, 1988

The earliest recorded blues singers of any significance were the women singing the blues in the early and middle 1920s. Harrison's book discusses the important singers except for Ma Rainey and Bessie Smith. She points out that these two artists have been covered in full-length biographies. In this instance I have alphabetized the book according to the author's name since the book covers multiple artists.

The book begins with an extensive section on the black theater circuit that employed the singers profiled later in the book. This is followed by a chronological history of these recordings. The author then offers detailed profiles of four singers of some importance and concludes with brief biographical sketches of other artists. Photos and record company advertisements enliven the text.

Many of the artists discussed are neglected or even forgotten today. This is partly because the blues revival has focused on mostly male country-blues singers who appeared on records about five years after the female singers began their recording careers. Harrison explains that the earlier female blues singers, with a few rare exceptions, didn't play any instruments and sang vaudeville and popular music as well as blues.

Harrison does an excellent job of examining differences in style among these artists. Ma Rainey, for example, was the earthiest and most rural of these artists, while performers like Alberta Hunter and Edith Wilson performed a wider variety of music and used language skills and sophistication to perform in France and England and even to appear on Broadway and in films. As the market for blues died down during the Depression, Hunter and Wilson were able to extend their careers through the 1930s through the variety of their musical skills. It is interesting that the artists who were successful in Europe, especially France, were generally light skinned and cosmopolitan and did not exhibit the earthy personal behavior of Ma Rainey or Bessie Smith.

The author also gives a vivid impression of what the TOBA (Theater Owners Booking Association) shows were like in terms of the exploitation of black performers and the various levels of musical and personal segregation that the artists endured. We also discover that although some of the women discussed, like Sippie Wallace and Victoria Spivey, did write songs, to a considerable degree these women relied on the work of Broadway and/or neojazz tunesmiths for their material.

This is a pioneering book. My only criticism of it is the author's failure to credit Bonnie Raitt's generosity in assisting Sippie Wallace in her performing and recording career during the 1980s.

19. *The Life and Legend of Leadbelly.* By Charles Wolfe and Kip Lornell. New York: Da Capo, 1999

Huddie (Leadbelly) Ledbetter was one of the giants whose work was a major influence on the folk music revival in America. This book is a full-length biography of his life and work.

Hollywood could scarcely invent a more colorful and complicated life than the one led by Huddie Ledbetter. Brought up by loving, financially successful (at least in relative terms) parents, he was unwilling or unable to endure the life of a black farmer in a racially segregated society. The book details his various imprisonments and provides the details about how his father was forced to sell off increasing sections of his farmland in fruitless attempts to keep Huddie out of trouble with the law.

Out of nowhere came John Lomax, who offered to employ Leadbelly as his personal chauffeur and assistant in his song-collecting endeavors. There is a persistent myth that Leadbelly sang his way out of prison, first in Texas and later in Louisiana. The authors show that Leadbelly did serve as a sort of occasional camp minstrel for Governor Pat Neff, but in fact he had virtually completed his term in prison when Neff pardoned him. One of the reasons that the governor remembered Leadbelly was that the latter sang a song that contained the words, "Governor Neff, if I had you, where you have me, on Monday morning I'd set you free." Taking no chances, Neff signed the pardon as one of his last acts as governor at a time when he was a lame duck and was not running for public office.

In Louisiana, the authors ferreted out the information that Leadbelly was pardoned because, counting some time off for good behavior, he had completed his sentence. As Wolfe and Lornell tell the story, after his release, Leadbelly signed a management contract that give John Lomax 50 percent of his earnings. When Lomax brought his son Alan along, because John found himself unable to relate to Leadbelly, the figure went to $66^2/_3$ percent.

The period when Leadbelly worked with the Lomaxes is a controversial aspect of the singer's life. Not only did the Lomaxes receive a generous share of his earnings, but one or both of their names appear on the copyrights of all of the songs that Leadbelly wrote, or at least received credit for writing. Over time, this would amount to a considerable sum of money since "Rock Island Line," "Goodnight Irene," and "Cotton Fields" all became major hit songs in recordings by various artists. Leadbelly also initially performed in prison clothes and even with a ball and chain. This undoubtedly represented John Lomax's attempts to dramatize the life of the ex-convict, but not everyone thought this to be an acceptable form of presentation.

The authors are evenhanded in presenting these conflicts, also not sparing Leadbelly for his occasional disappearances and his various ways of embarrassing Lomax. Eventually Leadbelly sued Lomax over his share of the royalties for the biography/songbook that Lomax was writing about him. A cash settlement followed recriminations on both sides.

Wolfe and Lornell go on to detail the last part of Leadbelly's life. Through his connections to Pete Seeger, Woody Guthrie, Josh White, and Brownie McGhee, Leadbelly became an important part of the folk community in New York City. The rest of Leadbelly's life was somewhat less colorful, although it was interrupted by one final jail term in New York in 1939. Numerous recordings and attempts to find a way into the movie community never really proved commercially successful. The authors then proceed to the final irony: less than a year after Leadbelly's death, "Goodnight Irene" became a major pop hit by the Weavers.

In a time when books by and about Woody Guthrie are appearing with almost alarming regularity, this book is essential reading for anyone who wants to know about the history of the folk music revival and the role of a major figure in that story.

20. *Alan Lomax: The Man Who Recorded the Whole World.* By John Szwed. New York: Viking, 2010

Alan Lomax was a key figure in folk music scholarship and the folk music revival. This book is the first full-length biography of this important figure.

Lomax started out in the world of folk music in the shadow of John Lomax, his famous father. John recorded music for the Library of Congress, and Alan began assisting him while he was still a teenager. John managed and traveled with Leadbelly after that artist's release from prison in Louisiana. Because John was a traditional white southerner, he and Leadbelly eventually came to loggerheads over issues of finance and behavior. John brought Alan on board, knowing that his more liberal political and social viewpoints would enable him to have better rapport with that artist.

Paging through the descriptions of Alan's career, even the most meticulous and hard-working reader will be astonished at the number of projects that Alan accomplished, along with the numerous other ideas that he had for songbooks, sociological studies, dramatic works, and radio and television shows. After two decades of collecting American folk songs, Alan moved to England in 1950, concerned about possible effects of the blacklist on his life and career. He had been involved with various radical organizations and had been active in the presidential campaign of Henry Wallace, and he feared being called to testify before various congressional committees. As Szwed explains, typically Lomax used this "exile" as a positive force, making a deal with Columbia Records to produce a series of recordings of music from various parts of the world.

Lomax's life in England, his flirtation with the skiffle music movement there, his return to the United States, and his development of cantometrics are detailed in this carefully written book. The study of cantometrics involved Lomax with a variety of other music and dance scholars, who attempted to organize world music styles around various social behavioral patterns. As Szwed explains, Lomax's ideas were controversial, and because he lacked a formal music (or sociological) background, there was much resistance to these notions by discipline-based scholars.

It all makes for a fascinating study, along with Lomax's involvement in the equally controversial area of music copyright. For example, it is laudable that Lomax had the Library of Congress pay his informants, but paying them the minimum wage that was available in the Deep South, for example, was not exactly generous compensation for their efforts.

What is lacking in the book is more explicit information about exactly why Lomax was such a controversial figure. As a personality, he tended to ride roughshod over collaborators in a way that Szwed minimizes in his discussion of the delta blues project. Although we get to know Lomax in the book, many questions remain unanswered. We never get to know Elizabeth, his first wife, as a human being, only as a sort of research assistant. Similarly, there is no real discussion of how or why his daughter Anna ultimately became involved in his work and became the keeper of his research legacy—all of this, mind you, after hardly knowing her father for a substantial portion of her formative years.

Alan Lomax was a unique personality with unusual gifts. This book will give a good notion of his importance in the history of American folk music.

21. *A Singer and Her Songs: Almeida Riddle's Book of Ballads.* Edited by Roger D. Abrahams. Baton Rouge: Louisiana State University Press, 1970

Arkansas singer Almeida Riddle's life spanned the era from the time collectors sought out folk informants to the time when traditional folksingers were sought out by summer camps and folk festivals. Roger Abrahams is a noted folklorist, famous for his work with African American youths in Philadelphia as well as his publications on traditional folk ballads. The bulk of this book consists of the collector simply allowing the singer to tell her life story and to discuss her songs and her choices of songs.

Almeida Riddle collected songs in notebooks, and this reliance on the printed word somewhat redefines the typical focus on the illiterate folk song informant. Riddle had strong notions of which songs she liked to sing and how the songs should be performed. She was not favorably inclined toward the folk song interpreters for whom songs become a vehicle for their performances. Yet Abrahams gently indicates the contradictions inherent in Riddle's performing songs before large urban audiences.

Each song is printed with the melody and information about how Riddle came to learn it. In a few instances, Riddle is the composer of the song. The songs seem to come from everywhere. We learn that Riddle is a relative of Frank and Jesse James and that Jesse himself was reportedly a fine singer. Other songs come from her own father, who was a vocal instructor, and her mother. Her uncles and cousins and grandfather also were sources for her songs.

Riddle had a hard life. Her father died young, and so did a number of her siblings and her husband, and for her, music was a refuge of almost religious proportions. While her husband was alive, she and he regularly sang together after supper. Many of the songs in the book are known today through other singers' versions, such as "Man of Constant Sorrow," which circulated widely through the movie *O Brother, Where Art Thou?* Some of the other songs are about local areas, like "Rome County" (in Tennessee). That song came to Riddle from folk song collector Joan O'Bryant. So this is an instance of the informant learning music from the collector!

Another interesting aspect of Riddle's work is that she was not a purist. For example, she describes how she had a lyric to a rather sentimental song called "Little Jim." She found the song in a poetry book and made up her own tune.

For the most part, Riddle liked to sing songs that told a story or hymns that taught something. She goes so far as to say that if a song doesn't make sense, "I probably won't learn it, or, if I like it, I'll change it in a way that make sense."

Abrahams confines his part of the story to the last thirteen pages of the book. He gives an interesting description of how Riddle is an artist as well as a tradition bearer, one who indeed brings her own individuality into the process of transmitting or revising a song. He points out that in a number of cases she knew particular songs but chose not to sing them.

We can thank Roger Abrahams and, of course, Almeida Riddle for illuminating the folk process of composition and revision as well as transmitting songs. This puts a more human spin on the role of the folk music informant outside traditional folkloristic notions about "the folk."

22. *How Can I Keep from Singing? The Ballad of Pete Seeger.* By David King Dunaway. New York: Villard Books, second edition 2008

This is a full-length biography of Pete Seeger, one of America's most renowned folksingers. Although there are several other books about Seeger, none is close to being as comprehensive as this one.

The original edition of this book came out in 1981 and was written with Seeger's assent but not with his active cooperation. Anyone who is even mildly familiar with Seeger knows that he is uncomfortable with mass attention and adulation. Over the years he came to appreciate Dunaway's book and decided to help him revise the book.

What makes this book stand head and shoulders above any of the other books about Seeger is that other authors tend to place him on a pedestal. Seeger is certainly a man of principle, with little direct interest in economic gain, and he was ready to go to jail rather than name names before the House

Un-American Activities Committee. What Dunaway brings out is the various struggles that Seeger has had between his idealistic beliefs and the harsh realities of communism and of the popular music world. An unlikely "star," Seeger is nonetheless a hit songwriter and recording artist. The author also reveals that he is a human being who is capable of outbursts of anger when his frustration level rises too high for him to control.

Disillusioned with the commercial success of the Weavers and with his efforts to galvanize the union movement with song, Seeger went through considerable soul searching before electing to spend his later years on a local cause, cleaning up the Hudson River. He also came to terms with his sort of inadvertently sexist lifestyle, leaving his late wife, Toshi, to handle his business affairs, organize his schedule, and manage other aspects of his life. It took him many years to realize that in this way he had acted no differently from many American males, depending on wives to give up their own career aspirations to take care of their husbands.

There are many interesting stories throughout the book. Seeger was involved with virtually every major figure in the folk music revival along with many lesser-known artists. Dunaway describes the mushrooming of interest in Seeger's *How to Play the 5-String Banjo*, which has sold over 250,000 copies but which, in its original, mimeographed form, sold all of one hundred copies in the first year of its publication.

Songwriter, song leader, moviemaker in collaboration with Toshi and his son Daniel, political singer, blacklisted artist, these are a few of the many aspects that Dunaway reveals about his subject.

Reading this book we see a person of many contradictions who has been a role model for espousing folk music beyond its commercial value. Anyone interested in the folk music revival should read this book.

23. *Man of Constant Sorrow: My Life and Times.* By Dr.
Ralph Stanley with Eddie Dean. New York: Gotham
Books, 2009

Ralph Stanley is one of the pioneering voices in the transition
between bluegrass and old-time music. This is his autobiography.

Like many of the pioneers in country music and in
rhythm and blues, Ralph Stanley grew up hard. He was born
in Spraddle Creek, Virginia, in 1927, just before the Great
Depression. His father left his mother for another woman
when Ralph was twelve years old.

Ralph and his older brother Carter were sustained by the
music. Their mother played clawhammer banjo, a pre-blue-
grass playing style, and as kids the brothers saw artists like the
Delmore Brothers and Bill Monroe doing local shows. Before
long, the Stanley brothers were playing on the radio, touring
wherever they could, recording for Rich-R'-Tone Records, and
selling their own songbooks.

As you follow Ralph's life, you begin to understand that
the roots of bluegrass and old-time music included a lifestyle
that the younger artists will never experience, just as younger
blues singers never lived the life that people like Charley
Patton experienced. As a result, Ralph is not especially fond
of the newgrass groups and their efforts to expand the base of
the music.

He is unsparing in his criticisms of these bands, and at
the same time he expresses great respect for Bob Dylan and
T-Bone Burnett. Ralph recorded a duet with Dylan, and the
O Brother movie and soundtrack album brought him a mass
audience that he had never previously known. It is sad that his
brother Carter never experienced this large an audience in
his lifetime.

If you want to know what it was like being a bluegrass or
old-time musician and how that music went from small venues

and small towns to major festivals and hit movies, this book is a great place to make that discovery. Many readers may not agree with all of Ralph's strongly held opinions about the music and some of the musicians who play it, but his sincerity and concern are apparent. It is too bad that the coauthor did not include an index, but fans of the music will find the book inspirational reading.

24. *The Mayor of MacDougal Street: A Memoir.* By Dave Van Ronk with Elijah Wald. New York: Da Capo, 2005

As I write this review, there is a new movie whose main character is loosely based on Dave Van Ronk. The movie was made by the Coen brothers, and the singer is named Llewyn Davis. In any case, this book is a memoir by folksinger and white blues artist Dave Van Ronk. It was put together by Elijah Wald, who is a writer, musician, and former student of Dave, from interviews and tapes. Van Ronk died in 2002, and Wald then pieced together and edited his reminiscences.

A fascinating, brilliant, self-educated iconoclast, Van Ronk's apartment was known as folk central during the key years of the folk revival. Van Ronk describes the scene in his typically colorful prose, sparing no fools. A walking contradiction, Van Ronk was one of the first white blues singers. With his asthmatic voice, his vocal growl fit into the idiom without his having to imitate specific black singers.

The book discloses how Van Ronk's music moved and grew over the years. Unlike most of his singer-songwriter colleagues, he deliberately limited the number of songs that he wrote. Casting aside his Dixieland jazz background, Van Ronk moved from specializing in blues to making his own arrangements of songs by artists ranging from Joni Mitchell to Kurt Weill.

Van Ronk offers many details if his early association with Bob Dylan. Initially, Van Ronk's first wife, Terri Thal, served as a manager for Dylan, and he often stayed at their apartment. When Dylan recorded Van Ronk's arrangement of "The House of the Rising Sun," Van Ronk was furious because he had wanted to record it first. His fury escalated when the Animals used the same arrangement and had a major hit with the song.

Incidentally, the book contains incorrect information about the copyright for that song. The *only* time that an arranger can copyright a song is when a song is in the public domain. That would have probably held true for "The House of the Rising Sun," and had Van Ronk copyrighted his version, he might well have received the large royalties from the songwriting credits on the Animals' recording. In any case, the friendship was never quite the same again, although the two made peace over that particular issue.

Van Ronk's politics were left-wing Trotskyite, but not Communist. He was the cocompiler of the satirical *Bosses' Songbook*, making fun of Communist and neo-Communist singers. Van Ronk also was one of the organizers of the late 1950s Folksingers' Guild, an attempt to form a union for folksingers in New York. That group did not work out, but years later the American Federation of Musicians organized a nongeographic local for folksingers called Local 1000. At no time in the book does Van Ronk refer to the musicians' union, which seems rather odd.

One of the charms of the book is Van Ronk's judgments. The reader may or not agree with Van Ronk's extravagant praise for Phil Ochs or his opinions on the worth of various other musicians. Having known Van Ronk, I can almost hear his amusement at readers' reactions to these opinions.

Lively, well written, and informative, this is a gem of a book.

25. *Can't Be Satisfied: The Life and Times of Muddy Waters.* By Robert Gordon. Boston: Little, Brown, 2002

Gordon's book is the result of a tremendous amount of research and interviews with an aging population of Muddy's musical associates, many of whom died during the research process or soon thereafter.

Gordon's book has aroused some controversy because he takes Alan Lomax to task for his treatment of musicologist John Work III during their Mississippi collecting journey. He points out that in Lomax's book *The Land Where the Blues Began*, Work receives a single mention. Since Lomax is a demigod in the folk music revival, any criticism of him is not taken kindly by his numerous associates, defenders, and relatives. But Gordon doesn't restrict his lens to Lomax's actions; he also points out that the complex relationship between Waters and Leonard Chess, co-owner of Chess Records and half owners of Arc Publishing, was essentially a recapitulation of Waters's early sharecropping days. Royalty payments were virtually unknown; rather, Waters would come to Chess when in need of money, and Chess, like a plantation owner, would then dole out some cash.

But this book is not all about conflict and rip-offs. Gordon offers a colorful description of Chicago's Maxwell Street "Jewtown" market, where musicians could make more money busking than they did working the South Side clubs. We see the side of Muddy portrayed in Jim Rooney's *Bossmen*, where he basically trains musicians to work in his band, knowing that they will later go on to establish their own careers and have their own bands. And Waters's house serves as a sort of blues headquarters, with other blues musicians staying there, eating there, and serving a critical role in the development of Chicago blues, much as Tampa Red had done in previous years.

Gordon is also quite willing to give Lomax credit for discovering and helping to promote Waters, and he also unveils his real friendship and closeness with Leonard Chess despite any financial travails between the two.

Muddy's tangled personal life included many romances, several wives, and numerous lovers, most of whom were barely, if ever, hidden from his wives. Through it all is the wail of the blues. It manifested itself in British tours, influencing a whole generation of major British rock stars, in the Chicago clubs, and later, finally performing for decent compensation as part of the folk revival of the 1960s. As Muddy puts it, "It took the people from England to hip my people—my white people—that a black man's music is not a crime to bring to the house."

Another fascinating detail is that Muddy could not read and could barely write. He signed contracts without having a clue about what they were really saying. Toward the end of his career, in 1973, he acquired a manager named Scott Cameron, who finally supervised his income from gigs, songwriting, and records. In a footnote, Gordon reports that Cameron tried to work out a publishing deal with Willie Dixon, but Dixon balked when he found that Cameron would own "one third" of the songs. The quote does not specify whether this includes both the publishing and songwriting share. The point Gordon is acknowledging is that although Cameron was certainly protective of Muddy's income and copyrights, no one is entirely altruistic! Waters himself was not generous with his band members, who eventually would leave partly for that very reason.

Muddy Waters was a major figure in the blues, influencing the British rockers and a bunch of white Chicago musicians like Elvin Bishop, Paul Butterfield, and Mike Bloomfield, and his songs continue to be performed by blues and rock artists. Gordon's biography paints the situation as it really was, without whitewashing Waters's business associates or Waters himself. It might have been useful to have a more detailed discussion of the equity of Scott Cameron's financial interest in his artists' publishing rights. This is left to a footnote, which details Willie Dixon's dissatisfaction with this arrangement.

26. *Josh White: Society Blues.* By Elijah Wald. Amherst: University of Massachusetts Press, 2000

Josh White was a major figure in both the folk song revival and the spread of the blues to white Americans. Wald has written the first full-length biography of this somewhat neglected figure.

Wald points out that White had a unique childhood, acting as the "lead boy" for blind blues singers from the time that he was eight years old. Since White had died by the time this book was begun, Wald interviewed White's family, friends, and associates in an attempt to get as many verifiable details as possible about this fascinating artist.

Nothing if not precocious, by the time he was fourteen years old Josh White was recording. Rectifying a well-circulated myth, Wald points out that White's first recordings were released under his own name. This was followed by two separate recording careers: one singing religious music under the name of the Singing Christian, and the other performing blues, using the name Pinewood Tom.

By 1933, Josh White had moved to New York, where he met and married Carol Carr. His career extended into several brief Broadway acting roles, performing on radio shows, and a number of appearances with the left-wing Almanac Singers, an informal group of musicians who at different times included Woody Guthrie, Lee Hays, Pete Seeger, Brownie McGhee, and Sonny Terry. Wald describes in considerable detail how White developed a sophisticated nightclub act that set him apart from other black artists of the day but at the same time tended to alienate fans who were in search of more "primitive" performances.

Wald offers many details of how the McCarthy period brought the blacklist to a number of folksingers. White took the position that he would testify before congressional committees and meet with the FBI, but he would not name associates as Communists. Wald conjectures that these inquisitors were a bit less aggressive with White than with some of his white contemporaries because they did not wish to be accused of racism. White was left in a middle position—he hadn't been a stool pigeon, betraying his friends, but he also renounced many of the causes that he had performed for or been involved in.

The author justifiably feels that Josh White has never gotten his due as a major figure in the folk song revival, attributing this to his sophisticated presentation and also to his turning his back on left-wing causes. Surprisingly, Wald hardly discusses Josh's unique guitar style. His mastery of rhythmic strums and particularly his use of string bends in many ways foreshadow the work of B. B. King. Much of this information is detailed in Jerry Silverman's master's thesis at New York University, which Wald does not reference in this book.

Songbooks and Folk Song Collections

For our purposes, a songbook is a collection of songs intended for people to sing and play. Folk song collections are more scholarly works, many of which contain detailed analyses of the music and lyrics of the songs.

> 27. *Slave Songs of the United States.* Edited by William Francis Allen, Charles Pickard Ware, and Lucy McKim Garrison. New York: Peter Smith, 1951 (original edition, 1867)

These African American songs were collected shortly after the end of the Civil War, largely in the Port Royal Islands of South Carolina. There are 136 songs in the collection. Each song includes both the melody and lyrics.

A good deal of what we know about black music during and before the Civil War derives from this publication. There was very little interest in the music of the slaves outside this book and a collection of spirituals by Thomas Wentworth Higginson, a colonel in the Union army.

Although the great majority of the songs here are religious, there are also secular songs, ranging from dance tunes like "Charleston Gals" to slavery songs like "Run, Nigger, Run!" In a number of instances, the authors provide short notes about the songs. For example, the song "My Father, How Long!" was sufficiently incendiary to Confederate adherents that "Negroes" singing it at the start of the Civil War were placed in jail.

A few of the songs remain familiar today, notably "Michael, Row the Boat Ashore," but most readers will find the bulk of the songs unfamiliar to them. Seven Cajun songs appear at the end of the group, which the authors describe as being sung before the start of the Civil War. All of them are in French and are printed without translations.

The importance of this book is that it gives the modern reader an opportunity to see what these songs were like without musical arrangements that attempt to modernize them. Since there is so little other material available from that period, it is difficult for a modern reader or critic to list any shortcomings that the book may have. The introduction at the beginning of the book comments on the use of language and other lyrical and musical aspects of the songs.

28. *Negro Songs of Protest Collected by Lawrence Gellert.* By Lawrence Gellert. New York: American Music League, 1936

Lawrence Gellert was a mysterious figure in the world of American folk music. After his doctors advised him to leave New York because he was suffering from "nerves," he moved to Tryon, North Carolina. He traveled all over the South, and this folio represents one of two folios drawn from his collection of African American music.

Gellert, who was white, set about collecting folktales and folk and protest music. In the introduction to the book, Gellert explains that he lived alternately in Tryon and in Greenville, South Carolina, "for more than a dozen years." Using a wire recorder, he traveled all over the "deep South." By 1936, he had collected over three hundred songs.

The songs printed in this folio, as well as in his later folio, are protest songs. Although such collectors as Howard Odum and Guy Johnson and the Lomaxes had collected a few such songs, few if any of them were as explicit as the ones that Gellert uncovered. Consequently, various collectors were suspicious of the authenticity of the songs. Moreover, Gellert did not document the sources of his songs. He claimed that the reason for this was simple: he was protecting his sources from violence by white authorities or racists.

For anyone interested in African American protest songs, this book and the companion volume, *Me and My Captain,* are essential reading. In the 1970s and 1980s, Heritage Records in England and Rounder Records issued long-playing albums of the songs that Gellert had collected. None of the artists was named, but clearly all of them were African Americans. This tended to refute some claims that Gellert had written all of the songs himself.

What makes the songs in this book stand out is the explicit nature of the singers' complaints and Gellert's. For example, in the song "Way Down South," the lyrics include the words, "White folk chase Nigger, like chasin' a squirrel." Most of the songs in this collection are unfamiliar ones.

However, "How Long Brethren" is basically a rewritten version of Leroy Carr's hit blues recording "How Long, How Long Blues."

The songs include melodies, lyrics, and piano arrangements by noted composer Elie Siegmeister. There is a brief introduction by Gellert, discussing the songs, and a short glossary of the terms used in some of the songs. It would have been nice to know the sources of the songs and where they were collected, but since Gellert has been dead for thirty-five years, this information will probably never be available.

29. *Wake Up Dead Man: Hard Labor and Southern Blues.* By Bruce Jackson. Athens: University of Georgia Press, 1999 (original edition published by Harvard University Press, 1972)

John and Alan Lomax collected numerous songs from southern prisons during the 1930s, especially in Texas. It was their contention that prison offered a culture that was frozen in time and that encouraged a "singing culture." Jackson's book consists of material that he collected in Texas from 1965 to 1969.

Jackson was aware that he was dealing with the musical fruits of a dying culture. Machinery had largely replaced the work of prisoners performing various farmland tasks together. Moreover, prisons later became integrated, and the African American work-song tradition was not shared by white or Latino prisoners.

Unlike the Lomaxes, Jackson concentrated on collecting music from a small group of informants in a particular place rather than traveling to numerous locations. He recorded prisoners singing, and he also talked to them in depth. The reader may also be surprised that he credits various wardens and prison officials for transforming and humanizing the Texas penal system. This involved making better food available for convicts as well as restraining the culture of brutal beatings practiced by prison guards.

All of the music was transcribed by Judith McCulloh and Norman Cazden. They adopted different methods of working. Cazden tended to transcribe the first verse while McCulloh offered more of a summary of what the prisoner was singing by examining the entire song. Both acknowledge the role of improvisation, which would make complete transcriptions unwieldy and quite lengthy.

As one of the convicts points out, you can "tell the truth about how you feel, but you can't express it to the boss." Jackson points out that the music isn't only about expression or feelings but literally sets the rhythms used by the men when, for example, they swing their axes.

Of all of Jackson's informants, he cites the creativity of one convict, J. R. Smith, in particular. Jackson describes Smith singing about everything that he observes—his sentence, the guards' weapons, and fantasies of going to other places. Smith is without a high school education, but Jackson is constantly amazed by his rhyming ability and his avoidance of repetition. The prisoners seem to be willing to be quite frank with Jackson. In "Mack's Blues," Mack Maze sings, "The boss packs a big horse pistol, and he think he bad, I take it in the mornin', if he make me mad."

Almost all of the prisoners were repeat offenders, many of them serving life terms. Their songs represent their hopes, their dreams, and resignation at their fate. The book provides us with a legacy of a lost time that isn't so long ago.

> 30. *English Folk Songs from the Southern Appalachians, collected by Cecil Sharp.* By Cecil Sharp. Edited by Maud Karpeles. London: Oxford University Press, second impression, 1952

Although this is a two-volume work, I am going to treat it as one book. The first volume consists of English ballads, the second of American songs, hymns, nursery songs, jigs, and play-party songs. Thirty-nine of the tunes were contributed by Olive Dame Campbell, but the rest were collected by Sharp and Karpeles.

Cecil Sharp was a British musician and folklorist who believed that if he traveled to relatively isolated areas of the southern Appalachian Mountains, he would find many traditional English ballads. In 1916–1918 he spent forty-six weeks in the mountains, collecting and notating these songs with Karpeles. She took down the words to the songs, and Sharp notated the music. The reader should remember that this was before the days of tape recorders. Both Karpeles and Sharp were concerned that they needed to collect these songs before the advent of technology and the building of roads did irreparable harm to traditional music.

Karpeles describes the instrumental tunes that they found as being of "little value." This is unfortunate, because quite possibly some of these tunes have subsequently disappeared. They simply weren't what the authors were looking for at that time.

The way that the authors worked was that they usually stayed at Presbyterian mission settlements and sought the music on foot. Sharp describes the mountaineers as friendly, religious, and more independent in spirit than their British contemporaries. The majority of his informants are described as being illiterate and their singing styles as being straightforward and direct, "without any conscious effort at expression." Oddly, Sharp encountered only one informant who played an instrument while singing.

Sharp had strong notions about musical validity. For example, he had seen John Lomax's book *Cowboy Songs* and described these songs as being inferior because "the cowboy has been despoiled of his inheritance of traditional song." In Sharp's eyes, traditional music was always preferable to music that evolved in a nontraditional way.

All of the songs are printed with lyrics and melodic lines. Many of them are printed in multiple versions, with texts and tunes that may differ slightly or substantially.

This was a landmark work that stimulated thought, discussion, and further fieldwork among folklorists and folk music scholars. As such, it is indispensable.

31. *Music for Patriots, Politicians, and Presidents: Harmonies and Discords of the First Hundred Years.* By Vera Brodsky Lawrence. New York: Macmillan, 1975

In this oversize, attractively illustrated book, Lawrence has gathered songs from American history. In this volume, she covers the period 1764–1876.

The bulk of the songs include texts but not melodies. In a number of instances, the texts are set to existing tunes. However, often these are tunes of the period, so knowing the name of the tune will not help the contemporary reader to identify that tune.

The book is organized by chronological periods in eleven separate sections. The opening section deals with the period just before the Revolutionary War. Consequently, many of the songs discuss taxes and prepare the ground for the forthcoming War of Independence.

The following section deals with the period of the revolution itself. There are tributes to George Washington, songs about various battles, and even a song commemorating Washington's crossing of the Delaware River. The focus in this section is on patriotic songs of the colonists. Successful battles are celebrated, heroes are lionized, and there is even a tribute to the gallant British spy, Major André.

As the book proceeds, it discusses various events in American history. Along with the text are reproductions of printed broadsides, woodcuts, and drawings. The political battles between John Adams and Thomas Jefferson are represented by songs favoring different sides of the battle. Some of the more interesting songs discuss Thomas Jefferson's alleged affair with his slave Sally Hemings. These songs are generally hostile to Jefferson, including such lyrics as "to breed a flock of slaves for stock."

The book continues with a collection of songs about various aspects of the War of 1812, the Mexican War, and numerous songs of the Confederate and Union soldiers during the Civil War. The last section includes songs that relate to the Reconstruction era, both those advocating for and against President Andrew Johnson.

Lawrence has put together an incredible treasury of songs from American history. It would have been easier for the contemporary reader to learn these songs if more of them included the actual melodies rather than directing the reader to tunes that are often obscure and difficult to locate.

32. *Songs of the American West.* Edited by Richard E. Lingenfelter, Richard A. Dwyer, and David Cohen. Berkeley: University of California Press, 1968

This book is as billed: a comprehensive collection of the music of the West. Each song is printed with lyrics, melody line, and guitar chords, except in instances where the authors could not uncover the tune.

The book begins with the gold rush era and songs about going to California or prospecting for gold. From there the authors move to songs of such occupations as stagecoach driving, working on the railroad, and so on.

On the bottom of each page are listed variants that the authors have found in various other collections of songs. I found the various songs about Chinese immigrants particularly interesting. Many of these songs are racist portraits of the Chinese, replete with phrases like "all your thieving clan," or "don't abuse the freedom you enjoy." Most of the songs about

Chinese Americans as well as a number of the other songs in the book are popular songs from the nineteenth century, not traditional folk songs.

A number of both pro- and anti-Mormon songs are also printed here. Other subject headings include songs about American Indians, army songs, mining and union songs, and songs of various occupations.

This is an excellent general collection. Although there are useful introductory sections for each part of the book, it would have been helpful to be able to read more details about each of the songs.

33. *The Folk Songs of North America in the English Language.* By Alan Lomax. Garden City, NY: Doubleday, 1960

Between them, John and Alan Lomax published four important collections of music from North America. This is the largest of their books, and this one is a solo work by Alan. The book contains 317 songs.

All of the songs include melody lines and guitar chords, and there are also one hundred piano arrangements of the songs. Headnotes for each song indicate the source of the song along with references that lead the reader to other versions of the song. There are also notes that discuss the songs at the beginning of each section.

The book is organized in an unusual way. The sections are separated by geography rather than subject matter. Part 1 is called "The North," part 2, "The Southern Mountains and Backwoods," part 3, "The West," and part 4 is titled "The Negro South." Each of these sections in turn has subsections that are organized by subjects, such as "Work Songs," "White Spirituals," and so on.

Since Alan Lomax spent his entire life collecting and recording music, this is an extremely comprehensive collection of songs. Murder ballads, work songs, square-dance tunes, just about anything in the English language is here. Since Lomax probably knew more than any other folk song collector about this music, the extent of the collection is breathtaking.

There are a few songs written by Woody Guthrie and Leadbelly here, but the great majority of the collection consists of songs that the Lomaxes or others collected in the field. The notes about the songs discuss where they came from and sometimes, especially with work songs, how they were performed.

Several prior Lomax collections, notably *Our Singing Country*, were significant collections of folk songs. The sheer size and scope of this book is why I have elected to include it in this book. Because the book was published in 1960, the discography includes LPs but not CDs. I hope that a future reprint will update this aspect of the book.

34. *Negro Folk Songs as Sung by Lead Belly.* By John A. Lomax and Alan Lomax. New York: Macmillan, 1936

Leadbelly had a number of unique qualities. John and Alan Lomax's book is a collection of his songs, his spoken recitations, and an account by John Lomax of his interactions with Leadbelly.

After the artist's release from prison, he acted as John's chauffeur and song-collecting assistant. This book is John's account of these interactions. To put it mildly, they did not go well. Initially, Leadbelly was obsequious and subservient, but later he became rebellious and even hostile.

The reader needs to understand that Leadbelly had very little contact with white people, and John Lomax, in turn, had little contact with African Americans outside his collecting work. In a rather strange arrangement, Lomax claimed half the income from Leadbelly's performances, and that amount escalated to two thirds when John's son Alan was brought on board to assist. Alan, being younger and more politically radical, had a better relationship with the singer.

Writing in the second decade of the twenty-first century, it is difficult to comprehend Lomax dressing Leadbelly in a chain-gang uniform or the singer's passing the hat at august locales like Harvard or folklore societies. Lomax accepts little or no responsibility for the rift between the two of them. From his point of view, it is all about Leadbelly's primitive needs, whether sexual or monetary.

Much of the value of the book comes from the song transcriptions. Leadbelly developed recitations to help explain the meaning of his songs to white audiences. The Lomaxes encouraged him in this endeavor. The recitations range from the re-creation of a railroad train ("Rock Island Line") to evocations of his growth to adulthood ("Fannin Street"). I can think of no other artist who developed these stories in quite this way, and looking at them in print is important, because on Leadbelly's recordings the words are sometimes difficult to understand. They also, in effect, create little short stories or novelettes around the songs.

Inevitably, the relationship between Leadbelly and John Lomax ended badly. The singer returned to Louisiana with his wife, Martha, and they ended up in lawsuits with John Lomax. Lomax paid off the singer, but in a sense has the last laugh because his and Alan's names appear as coauthors of the songs. Shortly after Leadbelly's death in 1949, the Weavers had a major hit record with his song "Goodnight Irene."

There aren't a lot of books about Leadbelly. In a sense, it's difficult to recommend this book because John Lomax always gets the last word, but the transcriptions of the songs are invaluable. They do not, unfortunately, include the names of the chords.

35. *The Blues Fakebook.* By Woody Mann. New York: Oak Publications, 1995

In this attractive nine-by-twelve music folio, Woody Mann has included the words, melodies, and guitar chords to over two hundred blues songs.

Many of the songs included were written and performed by classic blues singers like Bessie Smith or country-blues artists and songsters Mississippi John Hurt, Robert Johnson, Charley Patton, and Blind Blake. (A songster is an artist whose repertoire includes blues but who is not limited to that particular idiom.) There is also a sprinkling of songs by such later artists as Bo Diddley and B. B. King.

There are other collections of blues songs, but usually they belong to a specific music publisher. This book is more inclusive because the author has attempted to include songs by a variety of artists. In the introduction, Mann points out that some publishers refused permission to print songs under their control. Nevertheless, this is a sizable collection. Sprinkled throughout the book are some attractive and appropriate photographs by the late David Gahr.

The music to the collection includes only the melody lines and chords, as is generally the case with fakebooks. The reader will have to come up with his or her own guitar or piano arrangements. No headnotes appear with the songs, although quite a few of them will be familiar to blues fans through recordings.

In a number of cases, no composer credits are listed. Nor are the names of the publishers. This will prove to be a bit of an inconvenience for anyone seeking to make their own recordings of these songs. Still, if you are looking for a single source to expand your blues repertoire, this is a good place to begin.

36. *The Hell-Bound Train: A Cowboy Songbook.* By
Glenn Ohrlin. Urbana: University of Illinois Press,
1989

Ohrlin is a working rancher and former rodeo contestant
who has performed at numerous folk festivals, and he hosted
the Cowboy Tour sponsored by the National Council for the
Traditional Arts. In this work he has gathered a hundred cowboy songs, including both the words and the music.

Each song is introduced with information about where
Ohrlin found it, and often he includes details about how it
relates to his career as a rodeo contestant or his life as a cowboy. Examples of the author's drawings appear in various portions of the book.

There are basically several sorts of performers and collectors of cowboy song. Cowboy Jack Thorp (N. Howard Thorp),
whose collection of cowboy songs preceded the John Lomax
book, was himself a cowboy. Lomax was a folklorist with an
interest in finding and circulating cowboy songs. In the 1920s
and 1930s there were radio cowboys who spread cowboy songs
and lore through their radio broadcasts. There were also the
"movie cowboys," notably Gene Autry and Roy Rogers, who
sang around the campfire and on the trail in any number
of movies and, later, in the early days of television. Ohrlin is
someone who has been on the rodeo circuit and who has been
a cowboy and a rancher all of his adult life.

When Ohrlin prints songs and notes about the legendary bronc rider Pete Knight, he also includes a long discussion about Knight and his legendary career in rodeo. He
then prints three songs about Pete Knight, two of them by
Canadian western artist Wilf Carter and the third a fragment
of a song that Ohrlin collected from an old cowboy.

This collection is an excellent source of cowboy songs
for those interested in the songs or lore of the cowboy. A few
of the songs, like "Hallelujah I'm a Bum" or "The Strawberry

Roan," are well known, but quite a few of the songs, like "Lee's Ferry" or "Wild Horse Charlie," may be unfamiliar to the majority of readers.

Ohrlin is a reliable guide. He knows the composers of little-known songs, he knows many of the places and people that the songs are about, and he is both a collector and an informant. It would have been nice to have chords included with the melodies to make them even more accessible to the reader. The appendix includes an excellent "biblio-discography."

37. *Living Country Blues.* By Harry Oster. Detroit: Folklore Associates, 1969

The late Harry Oster was a college professor who collected hundreds of songs in the early 1960s while teaching at Louisiana State University. This book contains the lyrics to 221 songs and tunes to many of them as well.

In a sense, this book parallels the work of Bruce Jackson, whose book is reviewed elsewhere in this volume. Jackson was collecting prison work songs while Oster, at least in this book, was focusing on blues. Many, though not all, of Oster's informants were prisoners. Many of these songs were recorded by Oster for his Folk Lyric record label, and some of them have subsequently been reissued on CD by Arhoolie Records.

Oster spent a considerable amount of time with his informants. As was the case with Bruce Jackson, these informants developed sufficient trust in Oster to record some inflammatory lyrics about their working conditions and prison life. For example, prisoner Otis Webster has a spoken monologue in the song "I Want to Tell You, Bossman," where he says, "I hired for five days and a half, Now you tryin' to get seven day' here, that ain't right."

Oster's most famous discovery was Robert Pete Williams, serving a life sentence at Angola Penitentiary in Louisiana when Oster found him. Through Oster's intervention, Williams was able to get a pardon and later to travel and perform at various folk festivals and clubs. Williams was an especially creative blues artist, capable of making up songs almost instantaneously. Another example of an informant's trust in Oster is Williams's song "Yassuh an' Nosuh Blues." It includes the lyric: "Well, they treat me so dirty, they just don' know how to treat no black man. Boy, if they let the Negro alone, everythin' gonna be all right."

This is an important book because few folklorists were still collecting music by the 1960s, and when they were, they tended to focus on older, traditional material. Oster includes some older material by pre-blues artists like Butch Cage, but his focus is on blues.

If the book is ever updated, it would be useful to include an index. The only index in the book is by song title alone.

38. *Slave Songs of the Georgia Sea Islands.* By Lydia Parrish. Athens: University of Georgia Press, 1992 (original edition, 1942)

Lydia Parrish spent twenty-five years collecting songs sung in the Georgia Sea Islands. This book includes sixty of the songs that she found.

All of the songs include texts, melody lines, and descriptions of the singers and their songs. There are no chords given, but since this is essentially vocal music, this is not a serious omission.

The current edition includes a thoughtful introduction by musician/folklorist Art Rosenbaum. He offers some interesting contemporary insights into a previous foreword to the book, which had criticized Parrish a bit harshly for being somewhat sentimental and patronizing toward her black informants. Rosenbaum has a more hopeful attitude toward the continuation of the traditional singing found in the islands, which, he points out, persists today.

The book includes the original introduction by music critic Olin Downes. Sections on African survivals and songs listed by category comprise the rest of this work. Photos of some of the informants are spread throughout the book.

There is no question that Parrish's enthusiasm abetted the maintenance of traditional musicians, as did her financial support of some of the performers. Parrish describes the settings of many of the songs she has gathered. The Sea Islands have long been regarded as one of the last enclaves of African customs, largely due to their isolation from the mainland. By encouraging the singers and publishing their songs, Parrish made a major contribution to the study of African American music.

39. *Ozark Folk Songs.* By Vance Randolph. Edited and abridged by Norm Cohen. Urbana: University of Illinois Press, 1982

Vance Randolph was the primary collector of folk songs and folktales from the Ozarks. Some years ago, the University of Missouri Press reprinted his four-volume collection of songs from that region, originally published by the Missouri Historical Society. The current book is basically an abridged version of that collection.

Cohen points out that Randolph's collecting work began during the early 1920s, and he did not have any sort of recording device available to him. At first he took down the words with a pencil and then brought his informant to a house where someone had a piano and could transcribe the tune. Later he used a stenographer, and then he turned to a dictating machine.

Despite these laborious processes, Randolph was able to collect 1,635 texts as well as folktales. The book was originally published by the Missouri Historical Society, but as a result of some copyright controversies, copyright to the books was not renewed. The copyright law at the time protected works for twenty-eight years, and they were then renewable for an additional twenty-eight years. The books were not renewed, and so all of the books fell into the public domain.

In compiling this version of the collection, Cohen focused on songs that were related to the Ozarks by virtue of subject matter as opposed to including Ozark versions of songs found in other places. He also has elected to include only texts that include melodies. Cohen reprints Randolph's original introduction to the books. This is an interesting introduction to collecting techniques. When queries failed to produce any songs, Randolph would whistle a bar of two of the song and would stimulate the informant by telling him that he got a good tune from a neighbor. He would then deliberately make some musical mistakes in his singing, which would often stimulate the informant to sing the "correct" version.

The editor divides the book into eleven song sections, beginning with traditional ballads and moving to songs about specific subjects, "Negro and Pseudo-Negro Songs," and so on. Randolph's headnotes to the songs are preserved, and Cohen includes an updated extensive bibliography and discography of Ozark songs. Melodies to all of the songs are included, but chords are regrettably omitted.

This is one of the most significant regional collections of music ever published, ranking with the Frank Brown collection of North Carolina folk songs. It is a great source for songs and a wonderful source of information about music from the Ozarks.

40. *The American Songbag.* By Carl Sandburg. New York: Harcourt, Brace, 1927

At the time this book appeared, the only song collections available were written by folklore scholars, and they were not really intended for a general audience. John Lomax had published his book on cowboy songs in 1910, but *The American Songbag* was a much more inclusive book. Sandburg also had a reputation as a historian, poet, and folk song performer, and so he was much better positioned than others to capture a broader audience.

Today's folk song collections always include guitar chords and rarely have full piano arrangements. Writing at a time when the piano was the dominant instrument in American life, Sandburg included full, and often florid, piano arrangements of the songs by various musicians.

The book is divided into subject categories, such as "Pioneer Memories" and "Railroad and Work Songs." Sometimes the arrangement is credited to Sandburg himself; at other times, the person who did the piano arrangement gets that credit.

From the very beginning, John and later John and Alan Lomax functioned as editors of the songs that they printed. They combined texts of various versions and basically made artistic decisions of their own without consulting the sources of their songs. This also enabled them to copyright their versions of each song, something that became significant during the folk song revival of the 1950s and 1960s. Sandburg simply printed the versions that he learned, usually writing a paragraph about his sources. Some of the songs remain well known today; others are rarely performed in the twenty-first century. Sandburg also rarely goes into detail about other versions of the song. This invaluable collection includes ballads, mountain songs, blues, work songs, religious songs, cowboy songs, and a handful of Mexican border songs. Sandburg claimed that around one hundred of the songs had never been published before.

It is eighty-five years since the original publication of *The American Songbag*. The book is still in print, and despite the subsequent publication of many fine collections of songs, this book remains a major landmark in popularizing American folk music.

41. *A Song Catcher in Southern Mountains: American Folk Songs of British Ancestry.* By Dorothy Scarborough. New York: Columbia University Press, 1937

Dorothy Scarborough was one of the early and significant collectors of American folk music. This book followed a previous collection from 1926 called *On the Trail of Negro Folk Song.* The *Song Catcher* book represents three years of collecting and analyzing material, and the author died before editing the book, although the manuscript was complete. Two of her colleagues then edited the book for publication.

Scarborough traveled all over the southern mountains of Virginia and North Carolina, using a Dictaphone machine to record the music that she found. She relied on friends, contacts gleaned from other folklorists, and chance encounters. As happened with the Lomax books, often one informant or contact would lead to another, and Scarborough would then follow tortuous mountain roads or proceed as best she could on foot. An evening meal with a writer and teacher named Lillian Craig turned up ballads that Craig had collected, many sung by older informants.

Although Scarborough was primarily looking for American survivals of English ballads, she also encountered American-based items like a song with the lyrics:

> Jeff Davis is a gentleman,
> And Lincoln is a fool;
> Jeff Davis rides a milk-white steed
> Abe Lincoln rides a mule.

Occasionally the author contrasts American songs with their prior English version. For example, the African

American version of "Child Ballad 155: Sir Hugh, or the Jew's Daughter," never mentions the Jew and uses the term "cooling board," common to black songs but not present in the Anglo American versions. The latter invariably refer to the Jew's garden and the treacherous Jew's daughter, who kills the young gentleman.

The author also encountered the famous banjoist, singer, collector, and lawyer Bascom Lamar Lunsford, and he in turn traveled with her and helped her in finding songs.

There is an interesting Virginia version of "Green Grows the Laurel" called "Lovely Polly." This in turn bears considerable similarity to the song sung by Hedy West some thirty years later called "One Sunday Evening." In another Virginia song, "The Great Ship," the author prints a verse that is the same as the refrain of "St. James Infirmary." The appendix contains the music to seventy of the songs.

Collecting in the early 1930s, Scarborough was able to find a large body of songs in Virginia and North Carolina. Without her work and that of her colleagues, many of the songs and versions of existing songs that she collected would not have survived. The author herself comments on this in the early part of her book, knowing that roads, print, and radio were "killing off" folk songs in their original form. One can only imagine what she would have thought about the widespread presence of the media and the Internet today.

42. *Talkin' to Myself: Blues Lyrics, 1921–1942.* By Michael Taft. New York: Routledge, 2005

There are numerous songbooks that include the words and/or music to blues songs. Taft's book is a massive collection of blues lyrics from the first days of recorded blues until just after the start of World War II.

First of all, the reader needs to understand that this book includes no music at all. The reader seeking music as well as lyrics can go to other works that I recommend here. The lyrics are presented in alphabetical order, following the last name of the singer. To understand the depth of this book, over 2,000 lyrics by some 350 singers are presented. Each entry includes a brief biography of the singer, the date that the song was recorded, and the number of the original recording, for instance, "Bluebird 4502."

There is no attempt to choose specific artists here. Virtually every idiom of the blues is included. There are songs about romance and about working conditions, dances, and bootlegging—in short, all the subjects that constitute the raw material of the blues.

The author provides a few mysteries of his own. How did he choose, for example, the lyrics of Bessie Smith's songs? He has included only about 30 percent of her recorded works. What governed his choices? There are no composing credits given. In some cases, the singer has composed the song; in other cases, they come from another source. In avoiding composer credits, Taft deftly avoids any controversies about the actual sources of songs by such artists as Robert Johnson.

All in all, this book is the ultimate source for transcriptions of blues in the period covered. As a source of blues poetry, this collection is unexcelled. At the same time, by side-stepping the issues of why specific songs were chosen and who the composers were, the author has left these controversies for the reader rather than examining them himself.

43. *Negro Folk Rhymes: A New Expanded Edition, with Music.* By Thomas W. Talley. Edited with an introduction and notes by Charles K. Wolfe. Knoxville: University of Tennessee Press, 1991 (original edition, 1922)

The current edition is a collection of 349 songs. The original edition had fewer songs and only a handful of tunes, but

Wolfe discovered more songs and many of the missing tunes in Talley's papers.

Oddly, Talley was actually a chemistry professor, and his interest in songs was a serious hobby rather than a professional interest. Although there had been some songs published in magazines before this book appeared, this was the first publication of black secular songs in a book. Talley was also one of the few black collectors of black music. His own musical talents were strong enough for him to have toured as a bass singer with a vocal group called the New Jubilee Singers. As was the case with other musical groups at the college, the purpose of the tour was to raise money for the college.

Talley's songs came from his collecting fieldwork, and also from his own childhood repertoire. Many of the songs were collected in Middle Tennessee, and Wolfe refers to them as a sort of neglected "black hillbilly music." The book itself is divided into thirteen sections by subject matter, for example, "Dance Rhyme Section."

Some of the songs will be familiar to readers through the performances of old-time music bands like the New Lost City Ramblers or white musicians like Grandpa Jones or Uncle Dave Macon. Others are probably songs that a white collector might never have heard. For example, "Stand Back, Black Man" has the verse:

Stan' back, black man,
You cain't shine;
Yo' lips is too thick,
An' you hain't my kin'.

For anyone interested in the connections between white and black string band music, this is an essential work. The late professor Charles Wolfe deserves a great deal of credit for finding many of the tunes for the songs and for adding a

first-line index and citations of other collections in which
these songs appear. Talley also compiled a large collection
of folk myths and traditions called *The Negro Traditions*. Wolfe
edited this book as well.

> 44. *The Frank C. Brown Collection of North Carolina*
> *Folklore: Volume V, The Music of the Folk Songs.* Edited
> by Jan Phillip Schinhan. Durham: Duke University
> Press, 1962

The two largest regional collections of American folk music are
the Ozark Mountain collection of Vance Randolph and this
one. There are seven large published volumes in this collection,
four of music and the others involving folklore and supersti-
tions. Choosing this particular volume was somewhat arbitrary,
but it gives some notion of the scope of this collection.

The other music volume, also edited by Schinhan, contains the music of the ballads. Two other volumes are devoted
to lyrics only. The book discussed in this review contains the
music for 550 songs whose lyrics were printed in volume 3 of
the series, plus an additional 128 songs that do not appear in
that volume. The introduction to the book discusses matters
dealing with formal music analysis, covering such details as
scales, meter, and structure. The appendixes also deal with
technical musical matters.

The book is divided into fourteen sections based on subject matter and followed by an even larger number of sections
that are children's songs. This is a bit misleading because the
first group of songs takes up 504 pages, with the children's
songs a mere fifty-one pages. The subject matter of the children's section is simply subdivided into more categories. The
headnotes for each song reveal the source of the melody. Below
the melody, the editor refers to similar melodies found by other
collectors. Only one verse of each lyric is printed because the
rest of it appears in the volume that contains lyrics.

Don't let the above paragraphs scare you off. This is a treasure trove of tunes. If you are seeking to expand your own repertoire or you want to run through some entirely or mostly unfamiliar songs, this book is an incredible resource. The sections include "Black Minstrel and Negro Secular Songs," "Satirical Songs," "Songs of Prisoners and Tramps," and so forth. This is simply a monumental piece of scholarship. There are a few puzzling aspects of the book. Why are no instrumental tunes included? Did the collection simply not value music unless it had lyrics? It is also irritating to see a collection of hundreds of melodies printed without chords. It places the songs in the context of a museum rather than a living document intended for folk music enthusiasts to use with their guitars or keyboards. This has come up with other books, but this collection is so massive that it is particularly irritating here.

In item number 526, "Dark Was the Night," the melody is not printed, but the editor says it came from a phonograph record that was never found. This is most likely the Blind Willie Johnson instrumental piece, which was also used by Ry Cooder in the movie *Paris, Texas*.

American Indians

Many of the books about American Indian music are limited to the music of a single tribe. Frances Densmore authored more than a dozen such books.

> 45. *Indian Blues: American Indians and the Politics of Music, 1879–1934*. By John W. Troutman. Norman: University of Oklahoma Press, 2009

For many years, the emphasis of the Bureau of Indian Affairs was on getting American Indians to assimilate into the prevailing white Anglo culture. Troutman describes how this assimilationist platform tried to keep American Indians from singing, dancing, or speaking in their own language.

Along the way, the author surveys various stereotypes of American Indians that have pervaded country music in particular. He shows how artists like Hank Williams, Tim McGraw, Hank Thompson, and Loretta Lynn have spread stereotypical images, from tomahawk-brandishing savages to sexy ladies in buckskin minidresses.

Meanwhile, the Bureau of Indian Affairs did its best to prevent tribal dances. As Troutman tells it, this opposition proved futile. New dances emerged and spread, and "Indianness" became celebrated through pow-wows, intertribal ceremonies that united various tribes.

A fascinating contradiction to the government's party-line approach were Buffalo Bill Cody's mid-1880s Wild West shows. The government allowed him to present American Indian war dances as part of these shows.

Despite these conflicts and their generally unacceptable living conditions, the Lakota Sioux wrote a number of songs celebrating American Indian heroes in World War I. These were actually collected on the reservations through the 1960s, and the author prints a few of the texts.

Troutman summarizes the governmental restrictions by reprinting a 1923 message from the commissioner of Indian Affairs. It is addressed to "all Indians" and warns against the performance of "certain dances." Indians were asked to restrict their dancing to approved performances! At the same time, Indians at reservation or missionary schools were encouraged to perform "western" music in the form of band, orchestra, and choral music.

The author discusses the interesting contradiction that during all of this assimilationist frenzy, ethnomusicologists, especially Alice Fletcher and Frances Densmore, had not only penetrated the Indian Affairs office but were busily engaged in collecting music on various reservations. Troutman describes how Densmore sometimes had to explain to her singers why the government attempted to forbid them to sing or dance while at the same time she, a white government representative, implored them to do exactly that. And there is the strange contradiction that Troutman describes where Densmore and Fletcher encouraged their informants to give up their lands and relocate.

The last section of the book describes the work of some formally trained Indian professional musicians and the change of policy that came when John Collier became commissioner of Indian Affairs under President Franklin D. Roosevelt.

This is an unusual book that goes a long way toward explaining the story of American Indian music in the twentieth century.

46. *Music of Acoma, Isleta, Cochiti and Zuni Pueblos.* By Frances Densmore. New York: Da Capo, 1972

This book is a reprint of a 1957 work published by the US Bureau of American Ethnology. It includes the music to eighty-two songs along with detailed analyses of some of the songs. In some cases lyrics are included, and in other instances the author simply explains what the songs are about. Frances Densmore was an ethnomusicologist who taught music to American Indians all over the United States. She also recorded and transcribed their music. She collected thousands of songs, recording them on wax cylinders, starting in 1907.

My choice of this book is somewhat arbitrary because there are twelve other books in the same series, covering numerous other tribes. This particular volume is divided into songs of the various pueblos, designated by their function. The introduction includes some information about the various tribes, their geographic locations, and the musical instruments that the author encountered. She also includes the names of the various singers.

Each song is followed by a brief musical analysis, which includes details on such matters as whether each verse uses an identical melody. Virtually every imaginable sort of song is included, ranging from work songs to healing songs. For the most part, Densmore does not include the complete lyrics of the songs, but there are some exceptions.

The last portion of the book includes comparisons of the songs printed with those of some "certain other tribes." These comparisons relate only to musical matters, such as pitch and rhythm, not to lyrics.

It is interesting that so many collectors of Indian music were women. Louise Fletcher, Natalie Burlin, Laura Boulton, and Helen Heffron Roberts were among Densmore's colleagues. This is even more remarkable when one considers that much of this work took place during the period 1890–1920, when access to Indian reservations was difficult.

Densmore was a pioneer. She was not the only ethnomusicologist who collected American Indian songs, but because of her work ethic and her ninety-year life span, she was the most prolific collector and author in this field. It is almost foolish to offer any criticism of her work, but readers should understand that she had little interest in contemporary songs, such as those connected to peyote rituals. She also focused heavily on the music and much less on lyrics.

The Immigrants

When immigrants came to this country, they brought along their music. Many of their songs involved comparisons between their lifestyles in their original home and in this country.

47. *A Singing Ambivalence: American Immigrants between Old World and New, 1830–1930*. By Victor R. Greene. Kent, OH: Kent State University Press, 2004

Greene focuses entirely on lyrics, and he extrapolates themes from an examination of the songs of European immigrants. With the exception of Chinese Americans, all of the groups that he covers are European.

After a brief introduction, which details some of the conditions aboard ships that brought the immigrants, the book is divided into nine sections. Eight of them cover Irish settlers, Germans, Scandinavians and Finns, Eastern European Jews, Italians, Poles and Hungarians, Chinese, and Mexicans.

Each group's reason for coming to the United States is somewhat different, but in general, settlers came because of difficult economic, political, or social conditions in their home countries. Most readers will not know any of the material covered except, possibly, those who come from some of the ethnic groups described above. Some of the material is eye opening. One song from an army recruiter tells his Irish audience that the more blacks are recruited to join the army, the less Irish American soldiers will be at risk.

Another interesting point that the author makes is that the various groups came to the United States with a greater or lesser amount of resources. As Greene tells it, Germans, for example, were better equipped to adjust to the New World than the Irish because the Germans were more prosperous on arrival here. This induced a more optimistic view of their lot in the New World.

Each community had its own musical traditions. For example, there were German American musical theater performances in New York in the late nineteenth century. The Norwegian violinist Ole Bull established a failed utopian colony in Pennsylvania, which was satirized in a famous song, "Oleana."

Eastern European Jewish songs focused on both dis-
comfort in the New World as well as its potential opportunities. The famous Jewish composer Morris Rosenfeld offered
laments on how hard families had to work to survive. Italians,
Poles, and Hungarians also presented life in the New World
as a mixed blessing, offering opportunity but also expressing
sadness at what was left behind. The Mexican American songs
express similar sentiments.

The Chinese probably endured the worst racism of the
groups portrayed here. In terms of language and appearance,
they were the least likely to melt in the fabled melting pot.

The songs of the immigrants reveal a world that appears
remote but remains relevant to the lives of today's immigrants
from Central and South America and Asia.

48. *Klezmer! Jewish Music from Old World to Our World.*
By Henry Sapoznik. Second edition, includes CD.
New York: Schirmer Books, 2006

Henry Sapoznik is an active musician who performs both old-
time string band music and klezmer music. This book is a history of the music and how it has been revived in the United
States.

The first half of the book is devoted to the history and
background of klezmer music. The author traces the roots of
the music to Europe and Yiddish-speaking Jews. Many of these
musicians immigrated to the United States, typically settling in
New York City. As we follow the way the music developed, we
see it infiltrating the Yiddish theater in New York, and we find
elements of the style utilized by Jewish Tin Pan Alley composers like Irving Berlin.

During the 1920s and 1930s there was a thriving business of klezmer musicians. The bands typically used a clarinet
player and a violin player, and sometimes the tsimbl, a ham-

mered dulcimer–like instrument. Drums, flute, violas, cellos, and basses were also utilized in some of these ensembles.

The author weaves his own story into this picture. His own grandfather was a cantor, and in early childhood he was expected to sing as well. Rebelling against this music, Sapoznik becomes an old-time mountain banjo enthusiast and player. On a visit to banjoist and fiddler Tommy Jarrell, Sapoznik has a revelation when the fiddler asks him, "Don't you people have your own music?" Sapoznik then starts what has become a lifelong love affair and occupation as a klezmer music collector, archivist, teacher, and musician.

Tracing the history of the music leads to one particular musician, clarinetist Dave Tarras. Tarras becomes a sort of fountainhead of the music, and the author, along with "converted" bluegrass mandolin player Andy Statman, each form bands and become active in reviving the music. The author's band, Kapelye, tours Europe and records several albums. Sapoznik also begins working as an archivist and founds Living Traditions, a nonprofit organization dedicated to the preservation of Yiddish culture.

There are many fascinating aspects of the klezmer revival. As with bluegrass and blues, various factions favor more innovative or more traditional music. The music is played worldwide and is especially popular in Germany, a bit ironic considering that it was the Germans who were responsible for killing many Jews and for forcing many others to emigrate.

Including the CD with the book was an excellent idea because the reader can hear the various musicians and groups that are discussed in the text. This is a fascinating story. At times the reader might want to hear a bit less about Sapoznik's own activities, which probably deserve a book of their own, and more about some of the other people, like

Statman or the various bands that have been active in the revival.

49. *Immigrant Songs.* By Jerry Silverman. Pacific, MO: Mel Bay Publications, 1992

Most collections of immigrant songs include little or no music for the songs. This is a songbook, and although background material about the songs is included, the focus in on the songs themselves. Each song includes the melody line, chords, and a simple piano arrangement.

The author has relied on contributions from various scholars and performers. The scope of the book is encyclopedic. There are songs from virtually every part of the world. The text for each song is in the original language, and just below it is an English-language text.

Although there are certainly exceptions, most of the folk music revival has paid little attention to songs from the various immigrant cultures. This book is not simply a songbook but a fascinating mirror of the lives of immigrants. Their attitudes vary from complaints about excessive American materialism to gratitude at the political freedom and economic opportunity to be found in their new home.

Sometimes the lyrics reflect homesickness or remembrances of family left behind. The Mexican *corridos* present a less-than-positive evaluation of the work opportunities available to Mexican immigrants and the prejudice that they encountered.

This is an astonishing collection of music. It would have been wonderful if a CD were available with the book because musical notation is not really sufficient to convey the music of all the various cultures represented. They range from Bulgaria to Haiti, to the Philippines, to Cambodia, and many other nations.

Spanish-Language Music in the United States

Mexican Americans constitute the largest group of Spanish-speaking people in the United States. However, there is a considerable Puerto Rican population in New York as well as a large group of Cuban émigrés in Florida. The books below deal with only the Mexican American group.

50. *Lydia Mendoza's Life in Music (La historia de Lydia Mendoza): Norteño Tejano Legacies.* By Yolanda Broyles-González. New York: Oxford University Press, 2001 (CD included)

This book is a biography of the queen of Tejano music. To this day, Mendoza is probably the best-known *norteño* artist who ever lived.

Born in Houston in 1916, Mendoza and her family moved to San Antonio. Mendoza toured with her family from the age of eleven. The book describes how she learned songs from cards that came with gum wrappers. Early in her career, she was the *only* female singer in San Antonio. Mendoza won a contest sponsored by Pearl Beer, which brought several other female singers to temporary prominence.

Broyles-González describes how Mendoza recorded her most famous song, "Mal Hombre" ("Bad Man"), at the age of seventeen. The author employs many direct quotations from Mendoza. A thorough student of her music, she describes how the accordion was introduced into Tejano music in southern Texas. The many German and Polish residents there brought it to the attention of Mexican ranchers.

As was so often the case with blues artists, Mendoza's early career was controlled by a patron, who "gave me nothing. But I didn't care, because part of what I am . . . he helped me a great deal."

Soon Mendoza became a radio star, and her initial one-year recording contract turned into a ten-year deal. Although

Mendoza's sisters were also talented, they did not have the internal drive to succeed that motivated Lydia Mendoza. Her own comment on marriage is that "my career was not cut off by my husbands." Her first husband was a shoe repairman whose income was seven dollars a week. As she became successful, her husband accompanied her on tours, and she was also able to provide some luxuries for her family.

Mendoza went on to teach at California State University in Fresno as an artist in residence. In 1950 she made her first trip to Mexico. The book also describes a subsequent trip in 1954, when the producer of the show insisted that she use mariachi musicians to accompany her. The audience booed the mariachis, who were fired after the first week. It is very telling that the producer did not believe that a woman accompanying herself on guitar could provide enough entertainment for a large audience.

Another interesting aspect of Mendoza's story is her description of a lively theatrical audience in the small towns of West Texas in the 1940s. She explains that when cotton began to be picked by machines, these theaters and their audiences evaporated.

Mendoza experimented with different tunings for her twelve-string guitar, tuning the third string in octaves, for example, rather than with two unison notes. She also tuned the instrument a fourth lower than normal twelve-string tuning. The Es, for example, were tuned to the pitch of B. The book prints the lyrics of a number of Mendoza's songs. The second half is the same text as the first half of the book but translated into Spanish.

Broyles-González concludes with an analysis of Mendoza's music and career. She points out that several of Mendoza's songs contradict Latin stereotypes about gender and sexuality. She points out that Mendoza's recorded accompaniments varied from big bands to button accordion ensembles, smaller groups that included her own twelve-string guitar work and a single other musician, and even mariachi backup.

Anyone interested in the history of *norteño* music and its most famous artist will benefit from reading this book and listening to the music of Lydia Mendoza.

51. *A Texas-Mexican Cancionero: Folksongs of the Lower Border.* By Américo Paredes. Urbana: University of Illinois Press, 1976

Paredes's book consists of sixty-six songs from the Texas-Mexico border.

The songs are printed with melody lines, lyrics in English and Spanish, and guitar chords. The author also presents some suggested guitar strums. After presenting a half-dozen "old songs from colonial days," a long section includes songs of border conflict between Mexicans and Anglos. Shorter sections follow, with the subject matter including songs for special occasions and romantic and comic songs. The last section includes the songs of the "pocho," whom Paredes describes as the ghetto children of migrants or the predecessors of today's Chicanos.

Each section contains introductory material that describes the material that follows. Since Paredes is one of the outstanding authorities on this music, these sections clarify the songs that follow. The songs about border conflict discuss Mexican military heroes and also include ballads that describe the conditions that Mexican immigrants face. Many of the songs, like "Kansas," express some fatalism about the trek that awaits would-be immigrants, the dangers of corralling runaway steers, and the ultimate success of the cattle drive.

Certain mannerisms appear in the songs. For example, it is typical for the singer to place himself in the last verse of the song and to bid farewell to his listeners.

Possibly the most famous of all the songs in this book is the ballad of Gregorio Cortez, which was made into a movie.

This long ballad details how a sheriff appears on the property of two Mexican brothers. He accuses them of stealing a horse and shoots one of the brothers. The other one, Gregorio Cortez, shoots the sheriff. This long ballad details how Cortez flees and evades capture by the dozens of Texas Rangers who pursue him. The ballad claims that the many rangers are terrified of this "single Mexican." Eventually, Cortez is captured, and again the singer inserts himself into the last verse and bids farewell to his listeners.

As Paredes explains it, these songs helped to establish Chicano consciousness and provided the singers and listeners with a feeling of solidarity and commonality of goals. This book is fundamental to an understanding of the music of the Mexican border.

52. *Música Norteña: Mexican Migrants Creating a Nation between Nations.* By Cathy Ragland. Philadelphia: Temple University Press, 2009

The author conducted her research for this book as a working journalist in Austin and as a folklorist in Austin and Seattle. *Música Norteña* focuses on the music of undocumented immigrants and includes interviews with important Mexican American performers.

In recent years there has been an emphasis on *narcocorridos,* drug-related songs that involve the smuggling of drugs across the border. Ragland points out that there are far more songs that involve *mojados* than drug-related songs. *Mojado* is the current term used in place of the word "wetback" to describe undocumented immigrants from Mexico. Ragland acknowledges that some of the songs about *mojados* also involve the smuggling of drugs, but she emphasizes that the *mojado* is regarded as an outlaw or rebel. As such, he is a hero confronting the Anglo culture and showing "bravery and self-sacrifice."

The author also raises the interesting point that an idiom that glorifies drugs has also clearly become a marketing opportunity for various record labels and their artists. In that sense, the *narcocorrido* has become marginalized as a true expression of resistance.

Although such artists as Los Tigres del Norte and Ramón Ayala are the public face of this music, there are a handful of key composers who have established the image of the *mojado* as "cowboy, rebel, bandit hero, and outlaw." As enemies of the United States, the protagonists of these songs are turned into heroic patriots.

Ragland also stresses that this is not the romantic, sanitized Mexican music that is designed to appeal to the middle class but rather epic balladry that suits the tastes of the working-class immigrant. Originally the music of the southwestern border states, this music has spread throughout the United States as immigrants have settled in different parts of the country.

The book includes musical transcriptions and lyrics of a number of songs. In analyzing why *narcocorridos* have gained so much more attention than songs about *mojados*, Ragland says, "Mojado songs are more widespread, more likely to be sung by community-based groups as well as popular recording artists, and more reflective of the real-life experiences of both the singers and the audience."

Música Norteña offers a window into the music of Mexican American undocumented immigrants. It is a valuable and fascinating study.

53. *Hispanic Folk Music of New Mexico and the Southwest: A Self-Portrait of a People.* By John Donald Robb. Norman: University of Oklahoma Press, 1980

Robb was the primary collector of music in Spanish, in New Mexico in particular and the Southwest in general. This massive collection of songs represents his life work.

Santa Fe is the second-oldest town in the United States, after St. Augustine, Florida, and in various parts of New

Mexico and south-central Colorado, there are people who regard their heritage as Spanish rather than Mexican.

Robb's book deals with both the people described above as well as more recently arrived Mexican Americans. The book is organized by song types, beginning with romances and moving through *corridos, canciós,* and so on. In many instances, Robb has printed more than one version of the same song. All songs are printed in both Spanish and English, with the Spanish-language texts on the left side of the page. Because Robb was a skilled musician who was the dean of the music department and the School of Fine Arts at the University of New Mexico, he has transcribed the melodies to all of the songs.

The subject matter of the songs varies from love songs to religious songs and to comments about such events as the Japanese attack on Pearl Harbor. The author also explains the differences between the various song types, sometimes based on the form of the song-poem and sometimes on the subject matter of the song.

The book concludes with sixty-two instrumental melodies as a kind of supplement to the hundreds of songs that appear in the group, and the author has added a handful of full piano arrangements to a few selected songs.

Although there are some other excellent collections of Mexican border ballads, Robb's work has succeeded in preserving the music of New Mexico that derives more from Spain than from Mexico. In some ways, this parallels the documentation of old English ballads in the southern Appalachian Mountains by Cecil Sharp and other folklorists.

African American Music

One of the richest veins of American folk music is found in African American music. Spirituals, gospel songs, work songs, blues, and tangentially ragtime, all of these are inventions of African Americans. There are literally far too many books to reference in a short volume like this. Here are a few of the essential ones.

> 54. *The Country Blues.* By Samuel B. Charters. With a new introduction by the author. New York: Da Capo, 1975 (original edition 1959)

Charters covers blues from its earliest days up through the early careers of Muddy Waters and Lightnin' Hopkins. The book includes biographical material on such artists and songwriters as W. C. Handy, Leroy Carr, and Blind Lemon Jefferson and surveys of specific styles, such as jug band music.

One of the virtues of Charters's books is that they are quite readable. If Paul Oliver tends to be a bit dry, Charters writes in a style not unlike that of Alan Lomax, expressing his excitement about his musical discoveries. He makes the useful point that a number of the female "classic" blues singers of the 1920s, like Mamie Smith, believed that they were bringing an air of sophistication to the music, while the songwriters who wrote their songs similarly believed that they were taking raw blues to the next musical and artistic level.

Charters's description of Blind Lemon Jefferson offers an interesting comparison between the art of Jefferson and the rough and "primitive" lifestyle that he lived. Charters also is quite clear on how artists like Jefferson were persistently cheated by both white and black agents, artist and repertoire personnel, and record companies. This was probably the earliest acknowledgment in print about a process that has subsequently become much better known.

The book's description of Lonnie Johnson attributes a premature artistic death to that artist. Charters had no way to know that Johnson would be rediscovered in Philadelphia and would live out the last phase of his career as a respected artist in Toronto. Similarly, it is not the author's fault that the major blues rediscoveries—Skip James, John Hurt, Bukka White, Son House, and the others—all occurred after Charters wrote his book.

Not surprising, given when the book was written, there are some errors. Charley Lincoln was Barbecue Bob's brother, not his friend. Charters doesn't reveal many of his sources. For example, how does he know that Blind Lemon had two children and lived in a brothel in Memphis? Samuel Charters was (and remains) caught up in the romance of the blues, and his book was a starting point for a considerable number of later blues scholars as well as dedicated blues fans.

55. *Sinful Tunes and Spirituals: Black Folk Music to the Civil War.* By Dena J. Epstein. Urbana: University of Illinois Press, 1977

Although the title of the book refers only to American music, this comprehensive survey of secular and religious music includes considerable material concerning music in Africa and the West Indies.

The book begins by examining reports of African music on slave ships and then in the West Indies, where most of the slaves were brought. Epstein is a meticulous researcher, as befits a librarian, and her sources include all sorts of obscure journals, biographies, historical works, and even novels.

She establishes the presence of African instruments that were brought on the slave ships and also discusses how the slaves mastered instruments, like the fiddle and the French horn, that plantation owners wanted them to use for the owners' amusement and entertainment. Some of these reports appear in other works, but no one has documented them in such detail. Some of the information comes from advertisements that seek the return of runaway slaves who had musical talents.

Many interesting details emerge in the course of the book. The author documents the music culture of Congo Square, in New Orleans. Many slaves gathered there in what limited recreational time was allowed to them, and African instruments and songs seem to have survived there. Epstein also offers a detailed discussion of the pioneering book by Allen, Ware, and Garrison, also recommended in the current book (no. 27).

One of the most useful portions of the book is the author's calm denial of folklorist George Pullen Jackson's attempts to trace all "Negro spirituals" to white camp meeting songs. Epstein points out that Jackson's theories are based on published music, and there were virtually no publications of black folk music. She adds that Jackson and his supporters had little or no knowledge of African music or of the limitations of music notation as a source for disproving the originality of the spirituals.

For the reader who wants to learn about the African roots of African American music and how the music itself developed, this book is essential reading.

56. *The Gospel Sound: Good News and Bad Times.* By Anthony Heilbut. Revised and updated. New York: Limelight Editions, 1985

Gospel music was the successor to the traditional African American spirituals, and this book is an overall history of gospel music. It includes details about the history of the music and its most important composers and performers.

Any work of this kind is bound to be somewhat selective, but Heilbut has certainly included the most important figures in the music. Only a few of these artists will be familiar to many of our readers, but by including some of the lesser-known but influential people in the music itself, the author has provided us with a history of the evolution of the music.

Starting with composer-musician Thomas A. Dorsey, the book moves through the various artists involved in the composition and performance of gospel. Heilbut offers a grim picture of the financial hardships that have afflicted most gospel artists. Relying on church offerings, performances in small venues, and constant traveling, this is not a life for the faint of heart.

As we travel along with the author on the gospel highway, we come to understand the emotional underpinnings of this music. Heilbut presents a vivid picture of the emotional elements involved in gospel performance. There is also the ever-present temptation for the leading artists to cross over into popular music, as Sam Cooke, Aretha Franklin, and many other gospel artists did.

Through reading this book, we develop a clear understanding of how the music has evolved from the early days of the twentieth century to a niche in the contemporary music industry. Reading about the hard life of even some of the more famous artists in this field enables us to appreciate the raw emotion and power of the music and how it, in turn, has been so influential in the beginnings and developments of soul music.

I hope that the author finds the energy for one last revision of this book that could bring us up to date with current artists and musical developments.

57. *Stars in de Elements: A Study of Negro Folk Music.*
By Willis Laurence James. Edited by Jon Michael
Spencer. Durham, NC: Duke University Press, 1995

Jon Michael Spencer reconstructed and edited this fifty-year-old manuscript after he received a copy from Rebecca T. Cureau. Willis Laurence James was a trained musician and folklorist who did fieldwork in the South Carolina Sea Islands, Alabama, Georgia, and Florida, starting in 1923. He taught college in Georgia and Alabama before settling in the Department of Music at Spelman College in Atlanta.

Because James was a classically trained violinist, his affinity for African American folk music was a bit unusual during the period in which he worked. He covers many aspects of black folk music, from street cries to secular and religious songs. He includes transcriptions of the music, although the editor points out that fifty pages of songs were missing from the manuscript.

In his introduction, Spencer seems to have overlooked one of the most significant aspects of James's book. In the late 1930s, Lawrence Gellert, a white collector, published two folios of songs that he collected in various southern states. Gellert was associated with left-wing causes, and the songs that he printed were protest songs about chain gangs, lynchings, and both specific and general events. For years, his work aroused controversy, aggravated by his feuds with various figures in the left-wing folk song/folklore movement. The basis of the feuds were suspicions that the songs were not authentic but allegedly written by Gellert himself. (See the sections on Gellert's folios.) Although John and Alan Lomax occasionally printed protest songs, they were relatively tame compared to the ones Gellert had found. Virtually all of the folklorists working in the period 1920–1950 were white, except for the Johnson brothers and John Work. These musicians concentrated on religious music. James includes a number of songs of protest and complaint that parallel Gellert's work. These songs include "Mother Is Master Going to Sell Us Tomorrow," a slave lament, "Get in the Union," "Captain Riley's Wagon," a song that describes the eviction of sharecroppers, "Col' Iron," a song about a man who is afraid to face the bossman, "Soun' Like Thunder," a complaining work song, and so on. Unfortunately, the year each song was collected is not in the manuscript. These songs are simply not found in the publications of other folklorists.

James also has a very balanced approach to the question of whether spirituals are originally white or black in origin. Note that he was writing at a time when scholars tended to favor George Pullen Jackson's notion that all spirituals descended from white tunes. Although later scholarship tended to discredit or at least mitigate Jackson's theory, at the time James was writing, these ideas were generally accepted by folklorists.

Spencer has done a real service in bringing this manuscript to light.

58. *Encyclopedia of the Blues, Volumes 1 and 2.* Edited by Edward Komara. New York: Routledge, 2006

This book is as advertised, an encyclopedia of the blues. In addition to hundreds of biographical listings, it includes articles on specific aspects of the blues and such related subjects as migration.

Each volume starts out with a list of entries, which in itself takes up thirty pages. Lists of artists, record labels, "cultural entities," song titles, and other matters follow. One hundred forty-one people contributed to the book, and their contributions are credited in each case. The index alone is two hundred pages long!

Although the bulk of the book consists of biographies, there are various articles about, for example, slide guitar, migration patterns, and regional blues scenes. All in all, this is an extremely comprehensive guide.

Despite my admiration for the depth of this project, there are a number of frustrating aspects of this book. The editors throw in some jazz, soul, and rhythm and blues figures but omit many others. I am at a loss to determine how these decisions were made. Even fringe rock and roll figures, like

Richard Berry, author of "Louis, Louis," make an appearance. This tends to overwhelm the reader and to confuse matters. Worse yet, with 141 contributors, one gets almost as many value judgments about the importance of specific artists or styles.

For example, Dave Van Ronk, who is one of the pioneer white blues revivalists, gets all of one short paragraph. Similar treatment is given to Jessie Fuller, whose very famous song, "San Francisco Bay Blues," is not even mentioned in the book. Larry Johnson, one of the few black musicians playing Piedmont blues in New York after 1950, gets all of three lines. How did Louis Jordan get into this book?

This is one book that a blues aficionado can't live with or live without. If the book had focused more on blues and tried to be a bit less inclusive, it would have been a far more useful work.

59. *Black Culture and Black Consciousness: Afro-American Folk Thought from Slavery to Freedom.* By Lawrence W. Levine. Oxford: Oxford University Press, 1978

Although the title of this work doesn't include the word "music," in fact Levine includes a detailed analysis of the role of music in African American culture. He includes many song excerpts, but the book also offers much well-researched opinion and analysis about music.

He begins with a consideration of the role of African music, concluding that the music of black Americans is much closer to African music and the African American music of South America and the West Indies than it is to Western European models.

He goes on to discuss the use of music as a way of making life bearable for the slave, listing many early reports of slaves singing while working on plantations. Some of these reports come from the work of ex-slaves, some from white observers. Especially enlightening is the report of a white observer in 1870 who hears six different tunes set to one lyric in a church service. This observation is particularly valuable in light of the much later theories of white folklorist George Pullen Jackson, who maintained that all black spirituals derived from white hymn tunes. Clearly he did not take into account this improvisational nature of the music.

Levine prints various lyrics that relate to slave attitudes toward their masters; he also refers to lyrics collected by Guy Johnson that mix religious and secular sentiments in a single song. At the same time, he discusses the gap between religious and secular songs that made some singers, even convicts, loath to sing secular lyrics.

Possibly because the author sees music in social contexts rather than being committed to a specific point of view about the music, the author offers a number of interesting insights. In describing the difference between spirituals and gospel songs, he points out that "the latter increased the distance between the performer and the audience." The basis of the original form was expression, not the production of stars. Yet he also points out that the emotional expressiveness of gospel music in effect created a reaffirmation of the roots of the music.

There are also interesting discussions of the odd juxtaposition of minstrel music, derived at least in part from traditional black music, and the introduction of that music into black traditional song. The book then gives example of minstrel verses that were collected years later, as though they were folk songs. Levine sees the circulation of music through phonograph records as representing bearers and preservers of tradition. Many of the traditional folklorists saw these recordings as destroyers of the folk tradition.

The major contribution of this book is its insights about the meaning of black music in the culture itself.

60. *Black Song: The Forge and the Flame; The Story of How the Afro-American Spiritual Was Hammered Out.* By John Lovell Jr. New York: Macmillan, 1972

Lovell's work makes a good companion volume to Dena Epstein's survey of early African American music (no. 55). Lovell's book, however, is entirely focused on religious music.

Not only does Lovell discuss black traditional music, but he includes sections on various composers, arrangers, and performers of the music. These include such popular performers as Harry Belafonte, classical artists like Leontyne Price, and classical composers and arrangers who are both inside and outside of the tradition.

While Epstein dismisses the theory of white origins of the spirituals of George Pullen Jackson in a few paragraphs, Lovell provides a more detailed analysis of this notion. One of his main contentions is that Jackson simply did not analyze enough songs to make his case.

In his section of African music, Lovell cites ethnomusicologists and anthropologists in an attempt to prove that the music of the spirituals derived primarily from African roots, not from Anglo American camp meeting songs. He also casts doubt on the theory of Dr. Miles Mark Fisher, who contended that what most authorities have seen as references to heaven in the spirituals were actually yearnings for a return to Africa.

Lovell concludes that "the black spiritual is a folk song; the white spiritual is not." He provides discussions of symbolism in the spirituals, explaining, for example, that the words "Jubilee," "Canaan," and "campground" are all symbols for free land. He also points out that the number of black song collectors has been small, citing J. Mason Brewster as one of the few African Americans who collected black music.

The book concludes with an assemblage of twenty-eight scholars. Lovell queries them about the origins of the spirituals, how they spread, their subject matter, and what influence they have had on other musical styles. The scholars include historians, composers, and authors, from both the United States and abroad. It is interesting that the "jury" of scholars did not unequivocally support Lovell's insistence on African origins of the spirituals.

The book includes many lyrics of the spirituals as well as a discussion of the worldwide interest in these songs. Whether the reader agrees with Lovell's notions or not, this extremely detailed book is essential reading on the subject.

> 61. *Negro Workaday Songs.* By Howard W. Odum and
> Guy B. Johnson. Chapel Hill: University of North
> Carolina Press, 1926

Howard Odum began collecting African American music in 1905. This book is one of his two collections of these songs. It includes the lyrics of the songs and discussions of the subject matter. Fourteen of the melodies are printed in the appendix. This book appears here rather than in the songbook section because of its extensive use of sociological analysis.

The authors were sociologists, not musicians. Their primary interest in these songs was in the subject matter and what it revealed about the life of the singers. The book is organized by song categories: "Blues," "Songs of the Lonesome Road," "Bad Man Ballad and Jamboree," and so on.

One of the most interesting chapters is devoted to Left Wing Gordon. Gordon was an itinerant musician who had traveled to numerous states, working as little as possible and often being supported by women he encountered. He is, in effect, the archetype of such wandering bluesmen as Robert Johnson. Odum was so fascinated by Gordon that he later wrote three novels inspired by Gordon. Although other authors have mined similar territory, no one was interested in doing so during the 1920s.

This collection is about either work or work-related matters. The authors published a prior work that dealt with religious songs. Because the authors were not folklorists, they did not dismiss phonograph records as a source for the music, as many folklorists of that era tended to do.

The songs are printed in various lengths. Some are fragments, and some are complete songs. Among other things, the authors provide an analysis of how the blues they collected relate to or differ from similar material found on phonograph records. The authors are sensitive to thematic material, songs that relate to the life situation of the singers.

Anyone familiar with blues will be interested to find that some of the lyrics in this book appear almost a hundred years later in contemporary blues songs. The songs about jail life include such matters as prison sentences and laments about lost lovers. The work songs concern the boss (the captain, the worker's desire to leave, and the work itself). The songs tend to be matter of fact, although occasional glimmers of protest, like those found in Lawrence Gellert's collections, appear.

If you want to know what African American workers were singing in the early part of the twentieth century, this is a great place to find out about it. It is unfortunate that the authors didn't include more tunes in the book. You also have to wonder what life held for Left Wing Gordon after Odum left him.

62. *Blues Fell This Morning.* By Paul Oliver. New York: Horizon Press, 1960

Oliver selects a variety of subjects that are covered in blues songs, provides an introductory discussion of the topic, and then proceeds to print songs or fragments of songs that are subsumed under the particular subject.

The author has chosen eleven subjects to discuss, and he prints 350 lyrics that discuss these subjects. They include virtually every aspect of the blues, just as love relationships, working, magic, and jail.

Oliver, who is actually an architect by profession, was one of the first scholars to take the blues seriously, and he subsequently has written a dozen books about the blues. This book was the first one that printed blues lyrics extensively. Unlike the earlier folklorists like Howard Odum and Guy Johnson, Oliver's work involved studying and analyzing blues that were recorded on commercial recordings. Along with Samuel Charters, he opened up the field of recorded blues to serious analysis. The back of the book includes a discography of the blues that appear in the book.

Like many other subsequent blues scholars, Oliver minimizes the role of protest as an important aspect of blues music. Ironically, in the book he prints quite a few lyrics about jail, work, and other social issues. At least at the time he was writing, he doesn't seem to have been aware of the work of Lawrence Gellert, who was recording and compiling quite a few protest songs.

If you have a serious interest in the blues, sooner or later you will be reading some of Paul Oliver's books. This is a good one with which to begin your explorations. You should be aware that this book is about country blues, not electric blues or the white blues of the folk revivalists.

63. *The Kingdom of Zydeco.* By Michael Tisserand. New York: Avon Books, 1998

The author begins by clarifying the differences between Cajun music and zydeco. Cajuns are the people who were exiled from Nova Scotia in the eighteenth century and landed in Louisiana. Zydeco musicians are Louisiana creoles, people of mixed ethnic descent. Cajun music generally has the fiddle as its lead instrument, while zydeco usually features accordion and includes a metal rubboard that is played with fingerpicks in the rhythm section. The accordion is sometimes a single-row model, more like a concertina, or it can be a large piano accordion.

Tisserand's book is a detailed study of zydeco and zydeco musicians. We learn that there is a tension between the older, "purer" musical styles and some of the younger musicians, whose music is more inclusive of contemporary American musical trends. There is also, to an extent, a difference in objectives. The older music is local and dancehall centered, while the younger artists tour, even on an international basis.

We proceed on our voyage into the world of the Louisiana bayous and meet legendary musicians like Clifton Chenier and Queen Ida and important historical figures like Amédé Ardoin. Many of the musicians grew up in families where music is passed down from one generation to the next. So Clifton Chenier passes the torch on to his son C. J.

The music began in the form of house dances and then moved to clubs, some of which booked touring rhythm and blues acts as well as zydeco bands. As the music spread through such events as folk music festivals, it gained more of a national presence. Arhoolie Records and Rounder Records in particular recorded a number of zydeco artists.

There are some wonderful stories in this book. One of my favorites describes how Stanley Dural (Buckwheat Zydeco) is invited to play at the twenty-fifth anniversary of Island Records in 1987. Dural has his Hammond organ setup onstage and walks into a jam session with Eric Clapton and Ringo Starr, neither of whom know him. Dural plays an organ version of a solo that Clapton has just played, and they begin to trade off solos, each one building on the other. The audience of four thousand screams, and Clapton turns to Dural and introduces himself and asks, "Who are you?"

We learn how the music has spread through Paul Simon's use of Rockin' Dopsie's accordion on his *Graceland* album and the use of zydeco music in the movie *The Big Easy*. Many cities have non-zydeco musicians playing in zydeco bands from Denver to Portland, Oregon. Along the way we meet some of the younger, more crossover-oriented musicians like Keith Frank, Beau Jocque, and Terrance Simien. Tisserand makes for a wonderful tour guide, and he provides a useful discography in the appendix.

> 64. *Lost Delta Found: Rediscovering the Fisk University–Library of Congress Coahoma County Study, 1941–1942.* By John W. Work, Lewis Wade Jones, and Samuel C. Adams Jr. Edited by Robert Gordon and Bruce Nemerov. Nashville: Vanderbilt University Press, 2003

The authors combine music, sociology, and history in this collection of songs from the Mississippi delta. The songs are preceded and followed by two essays on the Mississippi delta and the position of African Americans in the delta during the period studied.

This project was begun at Fisk University, but for a number of reasons, the university asked for the assistance of Alan Lomax and the Library of Congress. The project's three principal researchers, musicologist John W. Work and social researchers Lewis Wade Jones and Samuel C. Adams Jr., all of whom were black, found themselves in a somewhat awkward spot working with celebrity and white folklorist Alan Lomax in an environment that did not welcome interracial social history projects.

Moreover, Lomax and Work simply did not get along. Lomax felt that Work was "lazy," and we can conjecture that Work probably felt misused and underestimated, and he was certainly aware that Lomax was not a trained musician and certainly would not have been able to do the musical transcriptions that Work made from the materials that the authors collected.

The facts of the matter are that the manuscript, which originally was supposed to be published in the mid-1940s, totally disappeared. Alan Lomax published a somewhat convoluted account of the trip in his 1993 book, *The Land Where the Blues Began*. The original manuscript of the present work was submitted to the Library of Congress, and it was misplaced, recovered, and misplaced again. Robert Gordon, one of the editors of the work, turned up Work's transcriptions and the other parts of the study in different archives and then, with Bruce Nemerov, edited the book into a coherent manuscript.

There are so many important aspects of this book that one hardly knows where to begin. This includes surveys of jukeboxes in Clarksdale, Mississippi, which reveal that the blues were only one musical style represented at the time. The scholarly essays by Jones and Adams reveal the nature of life in the delta, including details of working conditions, education, social change, and the history of the area. Work transcribed 158 songs, including spirituals, blues, work songs, ballads, and children's game songs. But this book is far more than a collection of songs.

For any reader who wants to know what the music of the delta was like in the 1940s, this book is essential reading. Inveterate fans of Alan Lomax may be disturbed by some of the editors' comments on the relationship between the researchers and Lomax, but the objective reader can make up his or her own mind on this matter. Because the original transcriptions were lost, the ones printed in the book come from microfilm versions in the Fisk University Library. They are readable, but recopying them would have made them more accessible.

Anglo American Songs

There are quite a number of books about country and blue-grass music that have appeared in the past few years. Many biographies and autobiographies are wonderful introductions to the music and its connections to earlier traditional music. Here are a few of the best and most readable books.

65. *Gone to the Country: The New Lost City Ramblers & the Folk Music Revival.* By Ray Allen. Urbana: University of Illinois Press, 2010

The New Lost City Ramblers played an important role in the folk music revival, introducing hundreds of them to the music that preceded bluegrass in Appalachia. They functioned not only as musicians but also as sort of semiprofessional folklorists (defined here as experts without college degrees in the subject area).

This is the first book that is entirely devoted to the careers of the various Ramblers, their achievements, their motivations, and the various interactions between the members of the group. It is an evenhanded look at the various conflicts within the group and how the band influenced several generations of future music makers. The original members of the band were John Cohen, Tom Paley, and Mike Seeger. Allen shows how the Ramblers were caught up in an odd series of contradictions and ambivalences. All of the band's original members came from a middle-class upbringing and developed a somewhat romanticized yearning for a simpler, more idealistic time and lifestyle. All of them were sympathetic to left-wing political notions, but the group made a calculated decision not to include political sentiments in their music. Since Mike Seeger's half-brother Pete was practically the crown prince of political folk music, this was particularly obvious in his case.

It wasn't only political folk music that the group avoided. They dedicated themselves to a sort of anti-pop-folk stance, scorning the Kingston Trio and other commercial groups. This stance was logical in terms of the members' own romantic attachment to a purer, simpler world, where marketing and merchandising were not something to be emulated or endorsed.

Allen is less secure in describing how the band's inability to make a living as a full-time performing group led to the departure of Tom Paley and the addition of Tracy Schwarz. The irony of this is that Tom's career as a math professor at Yale did not last. He subsequently moved to Europe, and of all of the Ramblers except Schwarz, he is the only one who dedicated his entire life to working as a full-time professional musician. John Cohen pursued his interests in photography and became a long-term, tenured college professor, and Mike Seeger spent much of his time collecting and recording traditional musicians.

Although Allen covers a good deal of ground in this book, he doesn't really delve into the question of the effects of the Ramblers' focusing so heavily on the music of southern whites. This wasn't important only in itself but resulted in a similar emphasis that goes on today with many of the so-called old-time music bands. This is not to say that the band was racist, but it simply ignored a major aspect of the American folk tradition. The reader is also left wondering about the various personality conflicts in the band. They initially seemed to involve Tom and John, and later Mike and John. Was this simply a matter of the typical performing artists becoming tired of constantly being together, or were there other grievances that the band members held against one another? Another recently published book, Bill C. Malone's *Music from the True Vine*, explores Mike Seeger in depth and provides some insight into these tantalizing questions.

66. *Strings of Life: Conversations with Old-Time Musicians from Virginia and North Carolina.* By Kevin Dunleavy. Blacksburg, VA: Pocahontas Press, 2004

A monumental survey of old-time musicians in Virginia and North Carolina, this book represents the fruit of fifteen years of research.

Dunleavy is a high school teacher, musician, and historian who spent fifteen years interviewing and playing with old-time musicians. There are other books that cover some of this territory, but no one, to the best of my knowledge, has spent this amount of time gathering details about old-time musicians.

The formal definition of folk music involves people learning how to sing and/or play in family settings rather than any sort of formal instruction. Dunleavy includes family trees that trace the roots of music making in various key families in the region. The great majority of the people interviewed in this book are relatively obscure musicians who were amateur or semiprofessional and who never tried to make a living as full-time musicians. The author includes many rare photos of his various informants, along with details about what tunes the various musicians played and any recordings that they made.

Although scholars have known for some time that there were many black musicians who played old-time music, this book documents just how many of these musicians there were, at least until recent times. There are a number of examples of black and white musicians playing together as well. Similarly, the book reveals that many women were playing music in these counties.

The author includes musical details about such matters as fiddle and banjo tunings and various unusual instrumental techniques. About a dozen tunes are also printed in music notation. Colorful stories about moonshine and the habits of various musicians also appear from time to time.

Anyone wanting an in-depth study of old-time musicians will benefit from reading this book. It is more like a book to dip into from time to time than something to read in a single sitting. The author doesn't present his own opinions or make an attempt to organize data in the way that a more formal folkloristic work might do. Although this may prove frustrating to academics, it is an interesting approach to the music, allowing the informants to speak for themselves.

Black and White

Some folklorists and folk song collectors have often given readers the impression that white and black musicians had little interaction, at least as adults. Here are some books that contradict this point of view.

67. *Music Makers: Portraits and Songs from the Roots of America.* By Timothy Duffy. Athens, GA: Hill Street Press, 2002

Tim Duffy started the Music Maker Relief Foundation in an attempt to provide financial security for older, indigent musicians. Most of these artists are relatively unknown, and Duffy provided not only financial assistance but also musical instruments and performance and recording opportunities for them. In this book Duffy tells the story of the foundation and the artists whom it has assisted. Numerous photos and a CD of the artists accompany the book.

After Duffy got his master's degree in folklore at the University of North Carolina, a chance meeting with blues artist Guitar Gabriel resulted in the beginnings of the Music Maker Relief Foundation. One thing led to another, and the network of financially impaired musicians expanded to include a number of other musicians. Financial support and encouragement from both anonymous angels and such well-known musicians as Eric Clapton, Taj Mahal, and B. B. King has enabled Duffy to continue the work of the foundation.

Most of the musicians you will meet in the pages of this book are not well known, rediscovered artists, although a few of them had achieved some notoriety in their careers. Frank Edwards had recorded during the 1940s and into the 1970s, Ernie K. Doe had one huge rhythm and blues hit, and Etta Baker was known by folk revivalists for her wonderful guitar playing on an LP recorded by Paul Clayton for Tradition Records. The artists cover many musical styles, ranging from blues to religious music and to country music.

The significance of this book and the work of the foundation is twofold. On one hand, it makes it clear that tradition-based music can still be found in various corners of the southern United States. Through the work of the foundation, the music was spread all over the United States and Europe through performances sponsored by the foundation and the CDs that it recorded.

For anyone who likes traditional music, this is a moving and fascinating book. It would have been useful if an index or table of contents provided a listing of the artists so that the reader could easily find them. This is a small omission in an important book.

68. *Folk Visions & Voices: Traditional Music and Song in Northern Georgia.* By Art Rosenbaum. Athens: University of Georgia Press, 1983

Art Rosenbaum is a visual artist and retired art professor who is also renowned for his excellent banjo playing and his activities in collecting songs and dances. In this book he profiles African American and white musicians in northern Georgia and prints their music.

The book includes photographs by Art's wife, Margo Newmark Rosenbaum, and also some of Art's paintings. Some of the paintings are of the musicians in the book, and some are more general, simply related to the subject matter.

In the introduction to the book, Rosenbaum describes how he began collecting music in northern Georgia in 1977. Although by that time many folklorists thought that traditional music had severely eroded, he says that "we found exceptional examples of all the important older forms, and at times these seemed to have grown in strength and beauty in the struggle for survival."

The author found some interesting examples of music cutting across color lines. The Wills and Barnes families had remained close friends during and after segregation. Jim Wills and Doc Barnes had worked together in the textile mills of Whitehall, Georgia. The two families sang and played music together in their homes. A photo shows the two families together, singing and playing.

Another interesting discovery is a black banjo player named Jake Staggers. He played for "both white and black dances, in churches, at corn shuckings and hog killings." According to Rosenbaum, Staggers was the only black banjo player in Georgia at the time of the publication of this book.

A final chapter discusses the famous white preacher, visual artist, and banjo player Howard Finster. There is also a charcoal drawing made by Finster included, along with four of his songs.

This book stands out for its integration of visual art with the text and for the interviews with the various artists. It is clear that the author developed excellent rapport with his informants. Chord symbols are not included with the music.

69. *Blacks, Whites, and Blues.* By Tony Russell.
Cambridge: Cambridge University Press, 2001

This is actually one of three books published in a volume
called *Yonder Come the Blues.* Paul Oliver edited a series of
books in 1971 for Studio Vista Books, and three decades later,
this book reprints three of them. The other two works, which
I will not discuss here, are Oliver's *Savannah Syncopators:
African Retentions in the Blues,* and Robert M. W. Dixon and
John Godrich's work, *Recording the Blues.*

Russell's book is an exploration of common elements
in African American and white music. Although this is a
relatively brief book, it is included here because it is really the
only work of any significance that considers this subject.

Reading books about white or black artists, one encounters occasional or repeated references to the interactions
between white and black musicians. The author has tried to go
deeper into the subject. He starts out with a description of min-
strelsy, which itself is a curiously hybrid musical form. Initially it
evolved from white musicians imitating, and sometimes making
fun of, existing black musical and dance styles. Black minstrels
infiltrated the process, and the music of both groups made its
way into southern musical styles of both groups. The author
cites numerous artists, songs, and recordings in whose work
one can hear this process evolving. Artists like Riley Puckett,
Uncle Dave Macon, Dock Boggs, and Jimmie Rodgers were
all white artists influenced by black and minstrel music. Frank
Hutchison was a white blues guitarist of some importance, and
the Allen Brothers were white artists who sounded sufficiently
black that Columbia Records mistakenly issued their early
records on their black "race records" line.

Russell also deals with the common stock of songs, like
"John Henry" and "Casey Jones," that were recorded by both
black and white artists. As the author points out, music tran-
scended segregation. The Carter Family, noted country artists,

traveled with a black chauffeur, Lesley Riddle, whose function was to memorize songs that the Carter Family encountered on their collecting trips.

Furthermore, there were incidences of black and white musicians recording together and also jamming together between takes at recording sessions. There were also the musicians like the Mississippi Sheiks, who played for white audiences as well as black ones. Jimmie Davis used black guitarist Oscar Woods, and some of Davis's songs used some of the bawdy lyrics found in blues recorded by black artists.

Possibly the most surprising thing about this book, and the one that highlights its importance, is that almost fifty years later no one has taken up the author's challenge to research this subject in depth.

Politics, Protest and Workers' Songs, and the Folk Song Revival

Folk songs include a wide variety of subjects. Protest music is music designed to protest against existing social conditions or to promote social change. Political music involves specific political issues, such as presidential elections. Workers' songs are songs that discuss working conditions in specific occupations. All of these categories may or may not interact. The term "protest songs" is often used to describe songs written by outside parties, such as union organizers, or people like Woody Guthrie, Pete Seeger, or Phil Ochs, who are not musicians and not workers.

70. *The Ballad Mongers: Rise of the Modern Folk Sound.*
By Oscar Brand. New York: Funk and Wagnalls, 1962

This is an overview of the folk song revival. Overall it is a balanced and fair account of the rise of folk music, covering the folk scene, especially New York, from the early days of the folk revival, featuring artists like the Almanac Singers, Marais and Miranda, and the Weavers through the peak of the folk-pop era and the popularity of Harry Belafonte and the Kingston Trio. Brand covers a lot of the bases, including copyright issues, purism, and the blacklist eras. He also raises issues that few have discussed, such as the notion of "red listing," where non-Communist artists like himself were not hired by left-wing organizations or promoters because of their politics.

The book has occasional inaccuracies, such as attributing Leadbelly's Texas pardon to the intervention of the Lomaxes, but overall it presents a reasonable portrait of the artists involved in the revival despite a lack of thorough scholarship. For example, Pete Seeger's father, if anything, was more political than Pete was, and he was hardly embarrassed by Pete's politics.

Certainly, the assessment of the importance of the Weavers in the early part of the revival is of importance to younger readers, who probably conceive of the revival starting with the Kingston Trio.

There is an interesting discussion of the storm that developed when Brand had a writer named William Cole as a guest on Brand's longtime WNYC radio show. Brand almost lost his show when Cole sang Nazi songs, which he had learned while a US soldier occupying Germany. Similarly, Brand was castigated on the right when he broadcast songs of the Castro forces and Algerian rebel songs. There have been very few discussions of censorship by the left in print, although current writers find denunciating the McCarthy era de rigueur.

As a long-term recording artist, Brand has collected and sung songs of the armed forces, something he discusses late in the book. Although some of his writings are necessarily dated (the book was written before the current copyright law was enacted), the discussion about the roles of informants, collectors, and performers of folk or folk-pop music and how they are compensated is still relevant today.

Amazingly, Brand's radio show is still on the airwaves today.

71. *Rainbow Quest: The Folk Music Revival & American Society, 1940–1970.* By Ronald D. Cohen. Amherst: University of Massachusetts Press, 2002

This is an examination of the revival from a historical-sociological viewpoint. Most of the existing books are either partially or entirely memoirs by participants. The author is a historian rather than a folklorist or a musician.

Cohen begins the book with a 1953 trip made by revivalist musicians Guy Carawan, Jack Elliott, and Frank Hamilton to the southern mountains. The three young musicians find some of their romantic illusions shattered when they encounter hostility, based on their style of dress, their supposed radical connections, and the very fact that they came from New York City.

In this way, the author sets up the history of the folk music revival. Steeped in radical unionism, promoting racial equality, and always singing and writing new songs, the Almanac Singers represented the generation of revivalists just before the three musicians above. This intrepid "band" of adventurers was a changing cast of performers, including Woody Guthrie, Lee Hays, Millard Lampell, Bess Lomax, and Pete Seeger. Brownie McGhee, Sonny Terry, and Josh White were also part-time participants. Sis Cunningham, Gordon Friesen, Tom Glazer, and Arthur Stern were among the other people in the Almanacs' orbit.

Cohen recapitulates the politics, the rise and fall of the Weavers, and the issue of blacklisting. These events are covered in more detail in Richard and Joanne Reuss's book (no. 76), but Cohen's book also delves deeply into the scenes that developed in Greenwich Village, Chicago, Boston, and Los Angeles. The success of the Kingston Trio led to mass popularity for the music, which in turn produced a sort of counterreaction to the more commercialized groups. The purists gathered in New York and Minneapolis, the latter scorning political music and the former crystallizing with the New Lost City Ramblers and with re-creations of traditional music and rediscoveries of traditional musicians.

Israel Young, proprietor of New York's Folklore Center, is the village skeptic, concerned at the degradation of the music into pop, railing against the contradictions inherent in popularizing the music, and serving a critical role as the headquarters of folk central. As Cohen points out, everyone went there. People bought books and guitars, had informal jam sessions, and engaged in furious political arguments, and friends and enemies were made.

There is a wonderful story about Bernie Krause, a young musician who later became the last of Pete Seeger's replacements in the Weavers. Bernie gets a gig at the Gate of Horn in Chicago and gets from Detroit to Chicago via freight train and hitchhiking. He finally hits the stage with Bob Gibson when two thugs come in, take him outside, and smash his guitar on the pavement. He then sees his grandfather, who tells him that no grandson of his will play in a den of whores and prostitutes!

There is a tremendous amount of information in this book. Stay with it, even though it may seem overwhelming. If you want to learn the roots of the revival and see where pop-folk and folk-rock came from, this book will point the way. Some scenes are inevitably omitted, like what was happening in such cities as Denver, Austin, Dallas, Oklahoma City, and Gainesville. The author might have better presented some of his information in text boxes or an appendix, because at times it does seem like an awful lot to absorb. In fairness, one book can't do it all. This was a complex and many-faceted scene, and covering it all might make for a book twice this size.

> 72. *Sing for Freedom: The Story of the Civil Rights Movement through Its Songs.* Edited and compiled by Guy and Candie Carawan. Bethlehem, PA: Sing Out Publications, 1992

Guy and Candie Carawan were active in the civil rights movement as song leaders and song collectors. The current work is a one-volume compilation of what were originally two songbooks published in 1963 and 1968.

The Carawans were based at the Highlander Folk School in Monteagle, Tennessee. The school's original music director, Zilphia Horton, was the wife of one of the founders of the school. When she died, Guy Carawan took on that position, beginning in 1959. The Carawans set out to record and popularize the songs that emerged in the movement.

Most of the songs include the melody lines, lyrics, and chords, with a few choral arrangements thrown in. There are also numerous photos that reflect the many people and situations that confronted the movement. A few of the songs are traditional, but many include new lyrics, and some of the melodies are also newly composed. For the most part, there are headnotes that explain the situation being described in the song.

This book is a veritable history of the civil rights movement. Sit-ins, demonstrations, jailhouses, and commemorations of fallen warriors are all here. This is an invaluable document for anyone studying the history of the civil rights movement. Most of the songwriters are not well known, but many of the songs are by people active in the movement, like Len Chandler, or people sympathetic to its aims.

Because this period included one of the most significant struggles in American social justice, this book is essential to understanding that struggle.

73. *Only a Miner: Studies in Recorded Coal-Mining Songs.* By Archie Green. Urbana: University of Illinois Press, 1972

Green has gathered together many recorded songs about coal mining and coal miners in this book.

Many folklorists have generally ignored recorded materials, scorning them as being commercial adaptations, revisions, or additions to traditional music. This book focuses on the subject matter of the songs rather than the alleged purity of their origins.

Green begins the story with the work of Pennsylvania folklorist George Korson. Korson was less concerned with the sources of his songs than with their subject matter. Green informs us that just as many folklorists self-censored any bawdy songs, Korson chose to avoid songs by any Communist informants. He was searching for the songs of the folk and therefore felt that songs of people coming from the outside were not useful to him. Therefore, he did not collect any songs from Aunt Molly Jackson or from anyone else who he felt was coming in "from the outside." And, like the already mentioned folklorists, Korson was not interested in collecting any bawdy material.

From Korson's work, Green moves on to survey race and hillbilly records that dealt with coal mining. Beginning with the 1908 recording of "Down in a Coal Mine" by the Edison Concert Band, he discusses the career of banjoist and former coal miner Dock Boggs. Boggs had recorded some mining songs during his early commercial recordings, but when he was rediscovered in the 1960s by Mike Seeger, the latter encouraged him to perform some of this material. Boggs even went on to create new songs about mining.

The author goes on to discuss songs that relate to coal-mining tragedies. He explains that these songs were generally ballads describing the events. The consistent volume of such tragedies led to the creation of various songs. The use of convict labor in the mines in itself inspired the creation of some songs as the miners massed against the use of convict labor and the destruction of their jobs. These difficulties came to a head in Coal Creek, Tennessee, where the miners had bitter fights with the Tennessee Coal, Iron and Railway Company. Green prints the song "Coal Creek Troubles," which was recorded in 1937. The song describes the use of convict labor and the role of the state government in fighting against the miners, ending with a wish that God help the poor miners.

An interesting aspect of the Coal Creek troubles was that the convicts were black and the miners white. This created some blanket assumptions about black workers being scabs and led to racially motivated antipathy between the two groups. Turning to more modern times, the author offers a detailed chapter on Kentucky ex-miner, master guitarist, and successful songwriter Merle Travis. Travis gained notoriety with his hit song "Sixteen Tons" and the many recordings of his powerful song "Dark as a Dungeon."

The book continues with a section on blues about the mines. This includes blues by such well-known black artists as Trixie Smith and white mountain singers like the Carter Family. A final chapter deals with mining songs and the folk music revival. Mike Seeger, Hedy West, and Billy Edd Wheeler are among the artists discussed here.

Green's work is important because he devoted detailed coverage to songs that appeared on recordings rather than to items collected by folklorists. It is also a thorough, sympathetic, and interesting discussion of songs of a particular occupation. In recent years, miners have continued to be celebrated by artists like Kathy Mattea and Darrell Scott, but these artists appeared and recorded after the publication of this book.

74. *American Folksongs of Protest.* By John Greenway. Philadelphia: University of Pennsylvania Press, 1953

This was the first serious study of protest music in the United States. It covers everything from protests about debtor's prison, songs of slavery, various strikes, and various protest singers, including Aunt Molly Jackson, Woody Guthrie, and Joe Glazer.

Greenway was the first person to discuss Woody Guthrie in detail and the first university-based scholar to devote serious attention to protest songs. He also was the first scholar to reference the work of Lawrence Gellert, a reasonably obscure figure by the time that Greenway's book was published.

If you are interested in labor history, this book is a veritable treasure trove of songs about strikes and union organizing. But the book isn't limited to union songs. There are songs about farm workers and sharecroppers, and many of the songs were written by relatively obscure figures, such as black composers John Handcox and Sampson Pittman. Although the book was written before the civil rights movement emerged, the author prints a number of songs about racial issues along with the songs about the struggles of farmers and laborers.

Some of the songs are printed with their melodies but without chords, and others contain only lyrics. In each case, Greenway gives the source of the song, and, unlike some other folklorists, he made no attempt to cut himself in on the copyright.

Greenway turned more conservative later in life, which is probably why he never attempted to revise this pioneering work. Although other books have subsequently been published that involve protest music, this is the basic work and the one that covers the most ground.

75. *Linthead Stomp: The Creation of Country Music in the Piedmont South.* By Patrick Huber. Chapel Hill: University of North Carolina Press, 2008

Through his profiles of four musical acts, the author tells the story of the music of the lintheads (cotton-mill workers). These four acts are Fiddlin' John Carson, Charlie Poole, Dave McCarn, and the Dixon brothers.

Huber begins with a description of the cotton-mill culture of North Carolina. From thirty-nine textile mills in 1860, the number escalated to 304 by 1906. Fiddlin' John Carson, the first artist profiled, was a former Atlanta textile worker who went on to become the first hit country-music artist.

The book describes how union organizers encouraged workers to sing on picket lines and even distributed printed versions of various labor anthems. The workers, in turn, wrote new songs for the struggles. Not only did Carson work in the cotton mills, but six of his children did as well. Although Carson walked out with other strikers, Huber shows how his politics were something of a mixed bag. He composed a racist ballad railing against the Jewish alleged murderer of Mary Phagan, and he joined the Ku Klux Klan. He also became a kind of house musician for Eugene Talmadge, the racist governor of Georgia. Yet Carson also performed with his wife and a son at an integrated benefit in 1933 for a Communist organizer. Possibly this followed the old cynical musician's notion that "a gig is a gig."

Mill hand Charlie Poole was an excellent banjo player who pursued a successful musical career, derailed only by his hard-drinking ways. Some of his tunes, like "White House Blues" and "Don't Let Your Deal Go Down," remain staples in bluegrass music today. When Poole settled in Spry, North Carolina, he found that the Carolina Cotton and Woolen Mills Company sponsored brass bands and string bands and that the company even financed a music-teaching program for the workers and their families.

The story of Dave McCarn is a bit different. His music, broadcast on local radio stations, dealt with working conditions in the mills. The songs "Everyday Dirt" and "Cotton Mill Colic" criticized the textile industry for its inadequate wages. Huber describes the bulk of McCarn's repertoire as being novelty songs that glorified drinking and partying. By 1929, the Loray Mill in Gastonia, North Carolina, experienced a strike, replete with antiunion violence and songs of social protest. The author details some of the protest songs of that time, which McCarn was not involved in. McCarn did write some sequels to "Cotton Mill Colic," but his songs did not result in any great success for him.

The last profile presented in this work is that of the Dixon brothers. The brothers were also former cotton-mill employees. Their songs, many of them written by Dorsey Dixon, varied between descriptions of cotton-mill life, like "Weave Room Blues," and religious songs. Dorsey's song "Wreck on the Highway," based on an actual event, went on to become a country standard in the country-gospel field. Huber also describes how Dixon was tricked into giving up half of his royalties by fellow musician Wade Mainer. The author recounts both of the Dixon brothers' participation in a strike at the Hannah Pickett Mill No. 2 and even entertaining at some strike rallies. Toward the end of his life, after many years of inactivity in music, Dorsey Dixon recorded a solo album called *Babes in the Mill.* It garnered positive reviews but was not a commercial success.

Huber's book provides excellent descriptions of the connection between work in the textile mills and the musical careers of its workers. He does a good job of explaining the contradictions between southern populism and religious and racial intolerance.

76. *American Folk Music & Left-Wing Politics, 1927–1957.* By Richard A. Reuss with JoAnne C. Reuss. Lanham, MD: Scarecrow Press, 2000

Although there are many books that discuss the role of the Communist Party and other left-wing organizations in the folk song revival, this is the most significant and detailed description of the politics of that era.

This book started its life as Richard Reuss's 1971 PhD dissertation in folklore at the University of Indiana. It was originally supposed to be published by Wayne State University Press in 1971, but the publisher apparently changed its mind because of the controversial nature of the subject matter. The present book represents some revisions that Reuss did before his premature death in 1986, together with considerable research undertaken by his wife, JoAnne.

The nature of the Communist Party's interest in folk song is a bit complicated. In the 1920s and 1930s, two streams of opinion developed about the way that folk music could serve the interests of the party. Classical composer Hans Eisler believed that music should be presented through the professionalization of workers' choruses. Originally he was supported in this notion by composer-ethnomusicologist Charles Seeger and by a number of American composers like Aaron Copland.

As the Reusses tell the story, two Communist organizers named Ray and Lida Auville began writing songs in a folk style in 1934 in Cleveland. Their notion was not to upgrade the musical consciousness of the worker but to write music that could readily be sung. Initially, the Auvilles had little support for their view, but when Aunt Molly Jackson, widow of a

Kentucky coal miner, appeared in rallies in New York, Charles Seeger, who had disliked the work of the Auvilles, was converted to the notion that the "music of the people" could be utilized as an effective political tool.

The Reusses detail this conflict, which, with the help of Alan Lomax, resulted in a victory for the folk faction and a defeat for the classical music enthusiasts. As the authors describe it, organizers in the textile and coal-mining industries went on to utilize the music of the workers in their organizing efforts.

The authors do an excellent job of describing how the various southern labor schools like the Highlander Folk School became centers for promoting the use of music as an organizing tool. Although the history of social protest music included the anarchist-syndicalist IWW songs and socialist songs as well, the Communist movement came to dominate this politicization of music.

The book also details how the so-called Popular Front movement tried to use music as part of the 1930s notion that Communists should unite with some of their left-wing political opponents in a common cause. By the late 1930s, the Almanac Singers in New York, a loose group of performers that included Pete Seeger, Lee Hays, Woody Guthrie, Millard Lampell, and Bess Lomax, were regularly performing for unions and at peace rallies. The temporary German-Russian nonaggression pact of 1939 induced the Almanacs to write and record a series of antiwar songs directed at Franklin D. Roosevelt. When Germany invaded Russia, the album was withdrawn, and the Almanacs went on to write a series of pro-war songs.

The authors detail the post–World War II history of people's songs and people's artists, the blacklist and its effect on various performers, and the role of music in the Progressive Party campaign of 1948. For anyone interested in the relationship of politics to the folk song revival, this book is required reading.

Miscellaneous: A Little Bit of This and a Little Bit of That

This is a category of noncategories. It includes books about children's music, collections of photos, and more.

> 77. *Cajun Music: A Reflection of a People, Volume 1.* Edited and compiled by Ann Allen Savoy. Eunice, LA: Bluebird Press, 1986

Ann Savoy is a performer and scholar of Cajun music. This book is a comprehensive guide to Cajun music and its performers. It includes the melodies, chords, and lyrics in French and English of the many performers portrayed in the book.

The author herself is renowned as a performer of this music and has interviewed numerous important figures in the music. In addition, the opening section of the book contains a brief guide to the various instruments used in the music. This includes the accordion and the fiddle, both of which are used in unusual ways in Cajun music. There is also a brief guide to rhythm guitar playing.

As the book progresses, we meet many significant figures in the music, like Dennis McGee, Amédé Ardoin, Iry LeJeune, and the Balfa family. The various sections trace the history and development of the music, from its early performers, through string bands and the "return" of the accordion and traditional fiddle players, to more modern Cajun songwriters. A handful of the most important zydeco artists are included as well.

Because the author is well known and respected in the Cajun music community and is married to a famous accordion builder, the interviews make for interesting and enjoyable reading. As each performer is discussed, his or her songs are printed after the interviews. Savoy has conducted the great majority of the interviews herself, but a few are contributed by other authors.

Photos of the performers or of matters associated with the music appear throughout the book. All songs are printed in both French and English. Because of the interviews, the reader gets a strong sense of how the music developed within French-speaking communities and within families. Many of the people portrayed didn't play music full-time or did so only for brief periods of time.

The author includes references to recordings by the various performers. Because the book was written before the widespread introduction of CDs, this discographical information is badly in need of revision. Such an undertaking would also enable the author to include some of the more recent artists who have emerged in the music in the twenty-seven years since this edition was published.

Such a publication would be a welcome event!

78. *Stagolee Shot Billy*. By Cecil Brown. Cambridge, MA: Harvard University Press, 2003

There are many versions of the badman ballad "Stagolee," often spelled "Stackerlee." Brown's book is concerned not only with the history of the ballad but with the actual story of the events that took place in a St. Louis bar that led to the song.

As the author tells the story, in 1895, Lee "Stagolee" Shelton shot a man named Billy Lyons in St. Louis. Brown traces the story back to a relationship between Stackerlee and his whore, whose name was Nellie Shelton. In the versions that Brown has traced, Nellie even offers to bribe the judge to get her man released, but the judge demurs.

Brown devotes considerable attention to Stackerlee's assuming the role of a proud black superman image, fearsome even to white policemen. Consequently, Stackerlee becomes a hero, the man who fears no one and is himself feared by the white power establishment.

According to Brown's research, the actual shooting was basically an act of revenge against Billy for a killing done by his stepbrother. That gentleman killed a friend of Lee Shelton. It turns out that Billy's sister was married to Henry Bridgewater, the owner of the saloon where the crime occurred. Bridgewater in turn went so far as to hire a special counsel to the state to ensure that Shelton was convicted of the crime.

Although Billy Lyons is invariably a pathetic figure in the many versions of this ballad, in fact, he himself was a notorious bully and thug. As Brown tells the story, the actual facts have been transposed in order to turn Shelton (Stackolee) into a sort of superpotent Super Fly character.

Not only has the author uncovered a great story, his details about the St. Louis political and social scene make absorbing reading on their own.

79. *The Erotic Muse: American Bawdy Songs.* By Ed Cray. Second edition. Urbana: University of Illinois Press, 1999

Dare we say that this book is an incursion into virgin territory? Many folklorists and folk song collectors censored bawdy material, and so this work stands somewhat alone in the folk song field.

Cray points out that Vance Randolph did collect 207 "unprintable" songs in his work. The State Historical Society of Missouri, however, would not allow him to include them when they published his materials. Other folklorists, like N. Howard "Jack" Thorp, self-censored their songs.

Some of the songs included in this collection, like "Six Nights Drunk," not only are published in other books but have been recorded by various artists. These other versions, however, are censored by the artist or collector. Many of the other songs here are simply not available in print or on records. Occasionally a song appears that is salacious but does not contain anything unprintable. "The Foggy Dew," basically a song of seduction, is one such example.

On of the most interesting aspects of this book is when the author takes a well-known ballad, like "Frankie and Johnny," and prints a large number of bawdy verses. Those readers who are familiar with blues artists will then realize that the recorded versions of these songs, although not entirely sanitized, only indicate the tip of the iceberg. In other words, an informal performance of these songs, as opposed to a recorded one, contains quite a few colorful and expressive lyrics that simply would not have been acceptable on records.

In the song "Stackolee," Cray's printed version details how the outlaw's girlfriend prostitutes herself in order to raise bail money for the outlaw.

Cray even reprints a lullaby that includes the lyric:

Today is the day they give babies away,
With every pound of tea,
If you know any ladies who want any babies,
Just send them around to me.

Other favorites, like "Hot Vagina" or "The Ring Dang Doo," are party songs that are explicit and whose subject matter is entirely bawdy. If these are songs that would appeal to you, then Cray's book is definitely the place to go. Each song is printed with the melody in music notation, and lyrics are included. Unfortunately, no guitar chords are included.

80. *Been Here and Gone.* By Frederic Ramsey Jr. Athens: University of Georgia Press, 2000

Frederic Ramsey Jr. is best known as the coauthor of *Jazzmen*, one of the first significant books about jazz. During the 1950s he traveled through Alabama and Mississippi with cameras and tape recorders. In this book, he documents his journey with photographs and text.

There are many people who have taken photographs of roots music and musicians. Ramsey's photos have a way of capturing his subjects in a natural, unposed way. The text of the book includes quotes and songs from his informants as well as descriptions of his journey.

Along the way, Ramsey encounters not only religious and secular musicians but also fragments from the brass-band tradition that preceded jazz. Many of the folklorists who made such journeys had little or no interest in this music because it was not folk music as folklorists would have imagined it.

Another attractive feature of this book is that Ramsey tells the stories of his informants but does not judge them, as so many of the earlier collectors were prone to do. For example, one of Ramsey's key informants was Horace Sprott, from Alabama. Sprott was sent to the county farm for shooting at a girl, whom he later married. They stayed together for eight years. Ramsey prints Sprott's evaluation of the situation: "Then, because he didn't want to kill her, he left her."

Sprott's story is that of the so-called roustabout, illiterate but able to retain a song after a single hearing. After wandering throughout the South, he returned to Alabama with a trove of work songs and ballads that he had absorbed in his travels. Sprott's music can be heard on Ramsey's Smithsonian collection of music from Alabama, but in this book Sprott describes *how* he learned the songs.

Ramsey also has a talent for printing blues lyrics that are above the ordinary. For example, one of Sprott's songs has the lyric:

> I asked the ticket agent, "Is my town on this road?"
> Ticket agent said, "woman don't you sit and cry,
> Your train blows at the station, but she keeps on passin' by."

For anyone interested in African American roots music, this book is a fine, nontechnical introduction with excellent, soulful photos.

81. *Hard Luck Blues: Roots Music Photographs from the Great Depression.* By Rich Remsberg. Urbana: University of Illinois Press, 2010

Midway in the Great Depression, the Farm Security Administration hired a number of photographers under the direction of Roy Stryker to produce a body of photographs throughout the United States and in Puerto Rico. The goal was to show the real and determined faces of Americans during this period of stress and struggle. The project did not focus on musicians, but many of the photographers were drawn to musicians and live music events. By 1943, funding for the project ended.

Many images in this book will be familiar to serious students of folk music or fans of the New Lost City Ramblers. The Ramblers used a number of FSA photos for their album covers, and Oak Publications, the leading publisher of folk music instructional books in the 1960s, used FSA photos throughout many of their publications. However, no one book has ever separated the music photos from the thousands of others in the collection. Prior to the publication of this book, the interested scholar or fan would have to go to the Library of Congress website, and I can testify to the fact that locating all of the music photos requires considerable digging through the collections from various states or subject classifications. What is even more remarkable is that through diligent research, Remsberg has actually been able to identify the people in the photos. Given that the book was written some sixty-five years after the last of these photos were taken, this is an amazing and laudable feat.

The author divides the photos by region, and there is a short introductory passage for each one. Going through the book brought several things to mind. The photos that are the most interesting ones are the ones that are least posed. They are not like promotional pictures of artists but show people in their home environment making music. There are photos of Salvation Army musicians, migratory farm workers, and even one of a "doped singer," taken by Ben Shahn in Scott's Run, West Virginia.

What readers think of the individual photos will depend largely on how they react to the musicians and how natural the photos are. There are indeed some photos that seem overly posed to me. Marion Post Wolcott seems to have been especially skilled at letting the musicians "breathe"; in other words, she was simply an onlooker snapping the photos while the musicians were playing.

One thing that struck me in looking at so many of these photos in one place was the lack of joy in many of the photos. This may well be a function of the period, when ordinary people were struggling for economic survival during a very trying period of American life. In any case, there is something here for those interested in blues, mountain music, New Mexican fiestas, prisons, and street music. In many ways, this book seems like a companion to Stephen Wade's book, *The Beautiful Music All Around Us* (no. 6). In that work, discussed earlier, Wade interviewed surviving musicians and relatives of musicians who had recorded in the 1930s for the Library of Congress. Remsberg's collection leaves the reader wondering what it would have been like if the photographers had been accompanied by recording engineers so that we could not only see their pictures but hear their music.

In a fascinating afterword to the book, musician-scholar Henry Sapoznik discusses how these photographs made by working artists contrast with the contradictions in Alan Lomax's role as "overseer and impresario" of the musicians whose music he collected and whose photos he took. Sapoznik goes so far as to say that Remsberg has a passion for the "images and the music culture they reflect," while he denies Lomax the ability to interpret the music that he collected. In this writer's opinion, Lomax did indeed have that ability, but he also had conflicting agendas, including his literal ownership of music and his need to reflect a political and, later, anthropological viewpoint.

82. *American Folk Songs for Children.* By Ruth Crawford Seeger. New York: Doubleday, 1975. Reprint of 1948 edition

Ruth Crawford Seeger was Pete Seeger's stepmother and the mother of Mike and Peggy Seeger. This is a collection of children's songs that she gathered while working at the Silver Springs Nursery School in Silver Spring, Maryland.

Seeger was a serious composer of modern music and also had done transcriptions for several books by John and Alan Lomax. She used her own children as assistants and guinea pigs in compiling this collection.

This is not, however, simply a songbook. It contains tips for getting children to sing and for developing activity games around the songs. Each song has suggestions for activities or group improvisation. Lyrics, melodies, chords, and simple but attractive piano arrangements are included for each song. Seeger also provides tips on piano accompaniments and suggestions for improvising words and activities that go with the lyrics of the songs.

The songs themselves come from different parts of the United States and from both the African American and Anglo American traditions. A few, like "Old Joe Clarke," will be familiar to most readers, but most of the songs probably will not be. Many of the songs are folk songs collected by more than a dozen folklorists, and others come from other printed collections.

Readers who have children will find this book an excellent source of repertoire. There are also a number of drawings by Barbara Cooney throughout the book. This is the essential collection of folk songs for children.

83. *Between Midnight and Day: The Last Unpublished Blues Archive.* By Dick Waterman. New York: Thunder's Mouth Press, 2003

Dick Waterman is a photographer who also had a career managing and/or booking a variety of blues artists in the 1960s and 1970s. His book has two essential components: the photographs that he took of the many artists whom he represented or encountered, and anecdotes about the artists and his experiences with them.

First of all, the photographs are emotional and in some cases rare portraits of deceased artists, and they also are suffused with a warmth that can only have come out of mutual respect between the photographer and the artist. The artists are shown in casual performances and also working at their craft.

The stories that Waterman tells transcend the hero worship that this sort of book often presents. As the reader goes through the book, it becomes apparent that there are artists for whom Waterman feels warmth and mutual respect, like Mississippi John Hurt or Robert Junior Lockwood, and there are others whom the author describes as being unreasonable, unreliable, or simply hard to get along with, like Luther Allison or Big Mama Thornton. Waterman is able to have respect for the artistry of a performer while going so far as to actively dislike him or her.

As someone who was involved in the music both as a fan and a businessperson, Waterman presents some astonishing stories of exploitation and wrongdoing on the part of white businesspeople toward black artists. The details of the exploitative relationship between Hill & Range Music and Arthur "Big Boy" Crudup are particularly offensive. But there are also the "good guys," foremost among them being Bonnie Raitt, who brought blues artists on tour with her and who consistently honored those artists who had inspired her.

There are very few failings that I can find in this book. It might have interested the reader to know that the owners of Hill & Range Music were themselves Austrian Jewish refugees from fascism. One of life's ironies, proving, I suppose, that sometimes the victim, freed from his tormentors, is capable of becoming an oppressor in his own right.

Folk Rock and Freak Folk

Folk rock represents the pop-rock evolution of folk music, starting with Bob Dylan in the mid-1960s. Freak folk, sometimes referred to as anti-folk or acid folk, is the contemporary version of punk- and New Age–influenced folk by younger performers.

> 84. *Seasons They Change: The Story of Acid and Psychedelic Folk.* By Jeanette Leach. London: Jawbone Press, 2010

Although this music intersects with folk rock, this book is more of a guide to the idiom that is today known as "freak folk." The difference between the two styles is that freak folk is more inclined to musical experimentation and New Age mannerisms rather than emphasizing the rock element of the music.

The artists discussed here are not necessarily obscure but are not major pop stars. The Incredible String Band, Vashti Bunyan, and Pearls before Swine, for example, are not artists who have enjoyed hit status in the pop world. Many of the artists discussed in this work will probably not be familiar to most readers. The Holy Modal Rounders, for example, were an East Coast–based "experimental" folk group, much of whose work was based on humor and enjoyment rather than the self-consciously serious singer-songwriter movement of the 1960s. Peter Stampfel of the Holy Modal Rounders remains a figure of some influence in the freak-folk world. The book also mentions quirky and creative songwriter Michael Hurley but doesn't bring his story up to date. Hurley continues to record and to perform, now living near the Oregon coast.

If the artists in this genre are somewhat off the wall, so are some of the record companies that released this music. Leach illuminates the world of ESP Records, who released the folk-rock psychedelic "band" the Fugs and who also recorded Tom Rapp's band, Pearls before Swine.

In a sense, this label functioned like the ultrafolk label Folkways, in the sense that label owner and attorney Bernard Stollman allowed the bands the creative freedom to record anything that they wished to. Like Folkways, paying the artists was a whole other discussion, one that Stollman didn't engage in. The difference is that Folkways never made any money from its recordings, while the Fugs and Pearls enjoyed excellent, if somewhat niche-market-like, sales. According to Leach, the first Pearls before Swine album sold somewhere between 100,000 and 250,000 copies. The discerning reader will recognize that this is a lot of "between."

The author gives a vivid portrayal of the spiritual aspects of psychedelic folk. As she reports in discussing the work of the little-known Collie Ryan, "Religious conviction underpinned dozens—if not hundreds—of privately pressed folk albums in the U.S.A." Along with this spiritual orientation was the presence of drugs, especially LSD. The world of early freak folk was a world that embraced the use of drugs as a way of achieving alleged enlightenment.

Many of the artists I have mentioned are relatively obscure American artists, and equal time is given to their British brothers and sisters, notably the Incredible String Band.

If you are seeking a guide to the origins of today's freak folk, Leech is an excellent cheerleader.

Her statement that Burl Ives's career was hurt by blacklisting is incorrect. Ives is one of the artists who admitted his Communist affiliations and named other artists to the US Congress. Consequently, he was able to go on to a very successful film career and a later career as a successful country artist. The author is also wrong about Moby Grape being denied hits because Columbia Records released five singles simultaneously. This was, in fact, a calculated plan devised by the label because it thought that there were no hit singles on the album. This did in turn create a buzz for the album, which supposedly sold half a million copies. Moby Grape's real problems were internal to the band and its members' lifestyle. In any case, chances are that this book will introduce you to dozens of unfamiliar artists.

85. *Eight Miles High: Folk-Rock's Flight from Haight-Ashbury to Woodstock.* By Richie Unterberger. San Francisco: Backbeat Books, 2003

In the mid-1960s, the folk revival went electric, with amplified instruments and drums. Unterberger describes how the music evolved during that tumultuous decade of social change.

Although most of the bands portrayed here are well known, the author also covers bands like the Beau Brummels and Blackburn and Snow, who were better known to musicians than to the general public. As the book describes, some of the lesser-known bands, like Kaleidoscope, were musically ahead of their time, featuring world music instruments and styles, integrating all sorts of roots-derived instrumental styles along with psychedelic jams. Unlike its competitors, Kaleidoscope did not use the LA studio session players known as the Wrecking Crew. Consequently, its records didn't sound like anyone else's. Unfortunately, this artistry did not translate into record sales.

The book captures the sort of experimentation and almost comedic madness that 1960s music making entails. When Columbia producer Bob Johnston encounters some rough patches with the moody artist Dino Valente, Bob spends two days in the studio with the band making paper airplanes and flying them around the studio. Unterberger does a good job of capturing an era that was living in its own time zone.

Many of the artists mentioned in the book have gone on to careers outside the world of bands. David Lindley of Kaleidoscope is a remarkable and versatile Los Angeles musician who plays a number of Eastern instruments as well as playing lead and slide guitar for such artists as Jackson Browne. By covering somewhat forgotten artists such as Tim Hardin, the book offers us a glimpse into the world of where this music came from and how it developed or disappeared.

Another aspect of folk rock was the Nashville influence. As a group of younger studio musicians emerged in Nashville, like multi-instrumentalist Charlie McCoy and drummer Kenny Buttrey, Bob Dylan and Joan Baez recorded albums with these musicians. The author shows the oddity of hippies and flower children coming down South and recording with the musicians who were, in their own way, rebels on the Nashville studio scene. This fusion of rock and country music was another aspect of the evolution of folk rock. As the author points out, some of the younger musicians who came to Nashville to record, like Steve Young and Jerry Jeff Walker, found that the Nashville sound was not suitable for the intensity of their work.

The British folk-rock movement also has a place in the history of this music, and the author discusses such groups as Pentangle and Fairport Convention, both of which made some inroads into the American pop scene but were more significant in England. The appendix to the book includes a reasonably up-to-date discography.

Unterberger covers all the major figures in folk rock, the Byrds, the Mamas and the Papas, Crosby, Stills, and Nash, and the rest, as well as artists whom the reader may not recognize. This is an excellent guide, only lacking some more in-depth coverage of the social world of and around all of these musicians. It is reasonable to argue, however, that that would make another book.

The Business of Folk

86. *Worlds of Sound: The Story of Smithsonian Folkways.* By Richard Carlin. Washington, DC: Smithsonian Books; New York: Collins, 2008

Moses Asch founded Disc and Folkways Records, which was the outstanding purveyor of not only American folk music but world music for many years. Carlin's book profiles the record company, the man behind it, and some of the major recordings that Asch published.

Motown Records in Detroit was famous as a company that utilized a production system that involved key record producers, studio musicians, and songwriters. Although Moe Asch never had any notion of turning his companies into corporate monsters, in a sense he operated somewhat similarly in the area of American folk music and world music, with occasional excursions into jazz.

Woody Guthrie, Leadbelly, and Pete Seeger were Asch's major, oft-recorded artists. John Cohen, Frederic Ramsey Jr., Mike Seeger, Harold Courlander, and various other folklorists and ethnomusicologists produced many Folkways recordings. Norman Granz briefly produced his Jazz at the Philharmonic series for Asch. Each LP had a booklet inside the album, often a fairly serious tome. This was especially true for the world music recordings.

Carlin documents how Asch's criteria for putting out a recording were unique to him. Did the recording have an authenticity of spirit, and was it something that he would want to retain on his catalog forever? Asch's golden rule was that anything in his catalog would never go out of print.

Among many, many other valuable recordings, Asch issued the Harry Smith *Anthology of American Folk Music*. Originally a bootleg recording, released without any authorization by the artists or their record companies, this six-album set documented American roots music. Although the immediate sales were not spectacular, practically everyone involved in the folk revival movement learned songs from these recordings. Artists like Mississippi John Hurt, Uncle Dave Macon, and Dock Boggs and jug bands, Cajun bands, and so on, were all represented in this recording. Carlin points out that it is key to understanding Asch's cultural orientation that he simply did not concern himself about the fact that he had no legal rights to these recordings. Clearly, the major labels had no interest in their own treasures of the 1920s and 1930s, so Asch put out the records anyway.

Carlin does a good job of excavating the many contradictions in Asch's character. A political radical, Asch recorded endless sessions with Woody Guthrie that were of no apparent commercial value. He put out a multi-album set of the music of Alabama. As the author states, he was able to do these things because he relied on library sales to bring in at least some consistent income and because his notion of paying royalties to artists was, shall we say, limited. When artists asked for money, he would pay them small sums, and he would pay people like John Cohen or Mike Seeger a few hundred dollars and no expense money to make their way down South and tape record little-known or rediscovered artists.

As the author explains, the remarkable thing is that the artists seemed more amused by Asch's financial wheeling and dealing than upset with him. He would indeed put out recordings not according to any logical schedule, but when he felt like it. Since many of the Folkways artists and producers saw themselves as rebels against corporate America, this system may not have intrigued them, but they accepted it.

The book includes many colorful illustrations, album covers, pages from the catalog, and other memorabilia. Folkways is now part of the Smithsonian Institution, and all of the records in the catalog can still be ordered and are produced on demand.

A fascinating story told in an appealing way by a writer and musician.

Folk Instruments and Instructional Materials

There are hundreds of guitar instruction books now available, along with quite a number of books for other acoustic instruments. I have culled a few favorites from a long list of excellent books.

Banjo

87. *Picturing the Banjo.* Edited by Leo G. Mazow. University Park, PA: Palmer Museum of Art, Pennsylvania State University Press, 2005

The Palmer Museum of Art assembled an exhibition depicting the banjo in 2006. This book is basically a catalog, with considerable text, that was intended to be read in conjunction with the exhibition.

The book itself is a handsome paperback volume, replete with reproductions of color paintings and black-and-white drawings and photographs. The text includes contributions by five other authors.

In addition to the wonderful reproductions of the paintings, the text discusses such matters as the original image of the banjo as an instrument popular in the slave era. There is also a generous sampling of photos of banjos in use during the nineteenth century.

Another interesting aspect of the book is the discussion of the use of the banjo in the late nineteenth century by upper-class white women. Paintings of white society women playing the instrument adjoin the text.

Later in the text, there are discussions of the banjo in the Harlem Renaissance, and a concluding chapter discusses the uses of the banjo today.

For anyone with even the slightest interest in the banjo, this book presents a very attractive introduction to its history and the social contexts of its use. It is also a visual treasure. The book is almost entirely devoted to the five-string banjo, and the reader should be aware that the banjo-mandolin, six-string, plectrum, and tenor banjos are virtually ignored in the text. This is unfortunate, because these are the instruments that were used in early New Orleans jazz and in jug bands. As such, they represent a significant portion of the history of the instrument.

88. *The Art of the Mountain Banjo.* By Art Rosenbaum. Pacific, MO: Mel Bay Publications, 1999

Art Rosenbaum is an excellent old-time banjo player who has also collected quite a bit of roots music. This book contains the music, written in tablature, for two LPs he did that are out of print. All of the tunes are transcribed in the book.

Many old-time music revivalists favor a single style of picking. For example, a school of players has arisen out of the so-called Round Peak style of clawhammer. Because Art has collected music from so many different sources, he doesn't favor a single style.

Art plays clawhammer banjo, but he also plays two- and three-finger styles that are the antecedent of bluegrass music. One of the things that sets this book apart is the extensive commentary about specific styles and the artists Art recorded who played in these styles. He is also fond of playing in a variety of tunings, which are explained in the book. Listening to the CD is also helpful because rhythms are probably more difficult to read than actual notes are.

Art is also a visual artist, and some of his drawings are included with the book, along with some photos taken by his wife, Margo Newmark Rosenbaum. Some of the tunes, like "Old Joe Clark" and "Arkansas Traveler," are apt to be familiar to readers. Others, like "The Green Beds" and "Harlan County Farewell Tune," probably are unfamiliar.

If you want to get a good grasp on old-time banjo picking, this book should provide you with lots of information about the strums and the tunings. There are a number of other books available about old-time banjo, but most of them are focused on specific styles or players. This book is a great place to start learning old-time banjo, and when you become more confident, you can explore some of the other books about specific players, like Wade Ward.

89. *How to Play the 5-String Banjo.* By Pete Seeger. Third edition. Beacon, NY: Oak Publications, 1961

Pete Seeger has enjoyed a long and rich career as a banjoist, guitarist, vocalist, author, and songwriter. The first edition of this book came out in 1948, and at the time it was virtually the only book available about the five-string banjo. Much of the terminology used today in banjo and guitar instruction, like the terms "hammering on" and "pulling off," seem to have originated with Pete Seeger.

Seeger's book is unique in the sense that he covers a multiplicity of styles rather than focusing on a specific technique. The book has several unusual features. Seeger begins with an up-picking style that is the opposite of clawhammer style. In many ways, his up-picking style is especially suitable for leading songs.

He then proceeds to teach clawhammer style, which he refers to as "frailing." He is also the only banjo player who teaches various strumming techniques that are adaptations of what tenor (four-string) banjo players do. The difference is that instead of using a pick, he shows the student how to do this with right-hand fingers or fingerpicks.

It's interesting to realize that sixty-five years ago he was teaching world music styles—calypso, a sort of flamenco playing, and even South American music styles. It seems as though today's banjo players are just now catching up with Pete's imagination all those years ago. Other practical suggestions deal with playing in 3/4 time and in 6/8. There is also a section on bluegrass and three-finger playing, which is somewhat sketchy and probably the weakest part of the book.

Everything is written in both music and tablature, and it's all readable, if a bit small. This is not the sort of book that you play through in a few weeks, but it should provide you with ideas and inspiration for many months.

90. *Masters of the 5-String Banjo in Their Own Words and Music.* By Tony Trischka and Pete Wernick. New York: Oak Publications, 1988

This is basically an instructional book that focuses on sixteen bluegrass banjo players and their music. It also contains information, but only a small amount of text, about sixty-eight additional players.

In the section on the "major players," each one is interviewed in some depth, and the authors print banjo tablature of a few of the artists' pieces. The people profiled are mostly major names in the idiom, like Don Reno, Earl Scruggs, Bill Keith, and Bela Fleck. There are also photos throughout the book of the various players.

Because the authors are themselves banjoists, the interviews focus on the stylistic mannerisms of the various players. This includes such matters as hand positions, individual musical trademarks of each player, and how they recommend neophytes learn.

The "other" players and the "big sixteen" are mostly presented in tables that describe what brand of banjo they play, how high they keep the bridge, their choice of tailpiece, whether they have ever taken lessons, and the age at which they started playing the banjo. Other details included are the gauge of strings used, capos, picks, and influences on their playing.

This is a valuable book for the serious banjoist but probably more than a casual player or fan needs. The title of the book is somewhat misleading because none of the profiles includes clawhammer players, minstrel players, or classical banjoists. A more accurate title would have been *Masters of Bluegrass Banjo*. Some readers may also find that the authors' inclusion of themselves among the sixteen major players is a bit self-serving. On the other hand, both of them are certainly well-known, credible players.

In general, I would recommend this book highly for the serious bluegrass banjo player. Other banjoists will probably find it less useful.

Dulcimer

> 91. *Appalachian Dulcimer Traditions.* By Ralph Lee Smith. Second edition. Lanham, MD: Scarecrow Press, 2010

The mountain dulcimer remains a somewhat exotic force in American folk music. This book is a short history and discussion of the use of the dulcimer in the Southern Appalachian Mountains. As Smith points out, the dulcimer is a relatively rare instrument compared to the guitar or fiddle. It also was somewhat localized; it might be present in a particular county but not known in a neighboring one. Typically, dulcimers have three or four strings, although the author has encountered a five-string dulcimer. Smith reports that dulcimers go as far back as the Renaissance, and similar instruments were played in Norway, Sweden, and Finland. Smith traces the American dulcimer to a German instrument called the *scheitholt*, which was brought to America by German settlers. He believes that German dulcimers were found in Virginia by 1818.

The book includes a generous sprinkling of photos of dulcimers and dulcimer players and biographies of a number of folk players. One of the turning points in the spread of the dulcimer was the popularity of Frank Proffitt, who was the son-in-law of dulcimer player Nathan Hicks. Proffitt became a bit of a celebrity because he was the source of the Kingston Trio's version of their hit song "Tom Dooley." Proffitt sold dulcimers but became overwhelmed by orders and farmed out the work to Leonard Glenn, who sold the instruments as "Proffitt dulcimers." Another artist mentioned is Jean Ritchie, who has concertized internationally, singing and playing dulcimer and guitar.

Just as songs change when learned by different people, dulcimer making has also evolved. Smith shows a dulcimer made by Homer Ledford in 1970, which has a widened body and fretboard. Folklorist Josiah Combs was a native of Kentucky who received a PhD from the Sorbonne. He taught at several American universities and played his dulcimer at various performances and lectures. Smith believes that Combs was the first person to perform with the dulcimer outside the mountains.

Toward the end of the book, Smith profiles some of the more modern builders of the instrument and then discusses variations on the traditional design. He also discusses the use of the dulcimer by black tobacco workers, who called the instrument the "coffin box." By 2009, Smith ran across a workshop by Bing Futch, who is of mixed Seminole and black ancestry. The workshop was on "Mississippi delta–style mountain dulcimer."

An appendix includes listings of Library of Congress and other recordings of the mountain dulcimer.

This book is an important survey of dulcimer history and style. The author has not delved into some of the more modern and adventurous dulcimer artists of the folk revival like Mark Nelson, Bonnie Carol, and the late David Schnaufer, who brought the dulcimer to Nashville recording studios. Clearly, the author preferred to focus on more traditional players.

Fiddle and Mandolin

> 92. *Mel Bay's Complete Jethro Burns Mandolin Book.* By Jethro Burns and Ken Eidson. Pacific, MO: Mel Bay Publications, 1993

Jethro Burns was part of the duo Homer and Jethro. They were known for their comedic skills, and many of their fans had little idea that Jethro in particular was a spectacular mandolin player. When Homer died in 1971, Jethro established a career as a mandolin player and began to write some books to teach aspiring mandolin players. This generous book, with two attached CDs, unveils the secrets of his mandolin technique.

Everything in the book is written in both music and tablature. The seventy-five tunes include a few old favorites, like "Cripple Creek" and "Mississippi Sawyer," but many of them are actually teaching studies, designed to expand the student's technical abilities.

I would estimate that going through this entire book could take well over a year for the average player. Burns includes such matters as double and triple stops, and he includes chords and chords on three strings. There are exercises designed to improve left-hand technique, especially the use of the little finger.

In later chapters, bluegrass and crosspicking are explored. Crosspicking is a technique used to simulate the sound of the bluegrass banjo and was popularized on mandolin by Jesse McReynolds of the bluegrass band Jim and Jesse.

The book is organized cumulatively; each section is a bit more difficult than the one before. Techniques like slides and pull-offs are introduced, as well as double and triple stops. The book includes some photos of Burns and a few humorous drawings. Toward the end of the book, some music theory is introduced, and the appendix includes four pages of chord charts.

This is not a book for the casual student but is an excellent tool for someone who wants to master a number of styles on the mandolin.

93. *The Phillips Collection of Traditional American Fiddle Tunes.* By Stacy Phillips. Pacific, MO: Mel Bay Publications, 1994

In this large book, Stacy Phillips has gathered together a collection of hundreds of fiddle tunes, including variations of some of the tunes.

These are not simply tunes that Phillips knows or has researched, but material that he has gathered from forty-four other fiddlers, including Ruthie Dornfeld, John Hartford, Tony Marcus, and Tim O'Brien. Since these fiddlers come from different parts of the country and play in a variety of differing styles, this collection is an impressive achievement.

All of the tunes are printed in music notation with chords. For those who read music, the book can serve equally well for guitarists, banjoists, and most especially mandolin players. Some compromises will need to be made for other instruments to compensate for fiddle bowings.

With each tune, Phillips lists the source of the tune, and he also provides performance notes where he considers that to be appropriate or necessary. Many of the tunes, like "Cindy" or "Devil's Dream," will be familiar to even the casual player, but one would have to be a human encyclopedia to know even half of the tunes listed.

This volume is devoted to hoedowns, breakdowns, and reels, while a second volume deals with rags, blues, waltzes, jigs, hornpipes, and polkas. Volume 1 should provide the fiddler with months of study or practice.

There are many collections of fiddle tunes. What makes this book special is the quantity of tunes and the number of sources that the author has used to compile this collection. Where fiddlers use modified tunings, the author has provided the notes for those tunings. Bluegrass, old-time tunes, and traditional tunes, they're all in this jam-packed volume.

94. *Kenny Hall's Music Book: Old-Time Music for Fiddle and/or Mandolin.* By Vykki Mende Gray and Kenny Hall. Pacific, MO: Mel Bay Publications, 2008

Kenny Hall is a living legend among musicians and fans of old-time music, the music that preceded bluegrass. *Kenny Hall's Music Book* is a generous sampling from the 1,100-plus tunes that constitute Kenny's repertoire.

Each tune includes a melody line, chords, and in the case of songs, lyrics. On the side of the page, the places where Kenny learned the songs are indicated, along with stories about the selections.

Although old-time music is generally associated with the Southern Appalachian Mountains, Kenny Hall has spent his entire life mostly around San Jose, Fresno, and Oakland. The music was popularized during the folk music revival by the New Lost City Ramblers but is today most prominent in the western United States, particularly on the West Coast. Kenny Hall has frequently been on staff at the Port Townsend Fiddle Tunes Festival in Port Townsend, Washington. In this role, he has influenced many far younger musicians.

The book is organized around subject themes: "Fiddle Faddle," "Rags, Tags and Wags," "Songs, Ballads, Ditties," and so on. The section titled "Kenny's Rambles" is particularly interesting because it ranges far afield. It includes Portuguese fado, Italian, Mexican, and Polish tunes.

Most readers will find the most familiar material in the "Songs" section. There are folk chestnuts like "The Big Rock Candy Mountain," tunes from the vaudeville era, cowboy songs, and ballads.

This book is essential reading for fiddle and mandolin players and other musicians seeking to expand their repertoire. Blind since birth, Kenny Hall is like a musical sponge, listening to everything and picking out the tunes that he likes best.

Guitar

95. *Mel Bay's Complete Country Blues Guitar Book.* By Stefan Grossman. Pacific, MO: Mel Bay Publications, 1992

This 259-page guitar instruction book comes with two CD's that provide an audio track for the music. All of the songs are printed in music notation and guitar tablature.

Stefan Grossman is a veteran blues guitarist who studied with the legendary Blind Gary Davis. He has written dozens of blues and ragtime guitar tutorials, and this is his single most complete collection. He includes country blues, open tunings, alternating bass, delta and Texas blues, and bottleneck guitar.

The introduction contains some useful information about the type of guitars that are ideally suited for blues playing, along with the names of shops that specialize in the vintage instruments that Grossman himself uses. (One of these shops, Jon Lundberg's, is no longer in existence.) Some other things discussed in the introduction include strings, capos, and fingerpicks.

Because the author has a very broad blues background, the pieces printed in this book in themselves represent a cross-section of blues history. Each selection is preceded by informative introductory text, which describes the history of the song and the specific playing techniques that are used in that song or arrangement.

Although there are any number of blues guitar instructional works available today, this one stands out for the number of styles taught in a single book, for the attractive photos scattered throughout it, and because the author has probably had more experience in playing blues than any other instructor.

This is not a beginner's book. It should provide months, even years, of practice before the student can learn all of the many techniques profiled and written. The book concludes with a discography of available recordings. All in all, a treasure trove of a blues guitar guide.

96. *The Art of Contemporary Travis Picking.* By Mark Hanson. West Linn, OR: Accent on Music, 1986

Merle Travis was the superb country-folk guitarist whose fingerpicking style influenced Chet Atkins and virtually every significant folk and country guitarist. Hanson's book is a guide to the style, its various patterns, and how to integrate the melody into the patterns.

Each song is printed in both music notation and tablature, and lyrics are included when songs are presented. It is worth mentioning that Hanson is a highly respected professional and teacher who performs widely and also teaches workshops around the country.

The book includes a CD, which is particularly useful for those who do not read music but is also a good tool to understand the rhythms of the strums. Most of the tunes will be fairly familiar to the reader, and the appendix includes a list of people who play in this style and specific fingerpicking tunes that these artists have recorded.

Many musicians who play Travis-style guitar use only the thumb and one finger. Not only does the author include the middle finger, but he is one of the few instructors who also includes some strums that utilize the third (ring) finger of the right hand. This in turn leads to a productive discussion on whether the player should rest one or more fingers on the top of the guitar while picking. The author prefers to keep his hands free, which enables him to utilize the ring and middle fingers of the right hand.

The author has written other useful books on alternate tunings and other guitaristic subjects. One of the things that I like about this particular book is the excellent printing job. The music and the tablature are all easy to read, and the instructional material is intelligently constructed and easy to follow.

The appendix includes chord diagrams and a short section on reading guitar tablature. This is a good book for anyone interested in Travis picking and exploring the use of more right-hand fingers.

97. *Sacred Steel: Inside an African American Steel Guitar Tradition.* By Robert L. Stone. Urbana: University of Illinois Press, 2010

Given the all-pervasive presence of the media, it is unusual for a new musical idiom to emerge and develop for years before it becomes widely recognized. *Sacred Steel* portrays the origins and development of the steel guitar as a musical part of the African American evangelical religious music universe.

Stone takes us to the two church denominations where this music emerged. They are the Keith Dominion, where guitarist Willie Eason was a major influence, and the Jewell Dominion, where guitarist Bishop Lorenzo Harrison was the major guitar stylist. Stone explains that Harrison's repertoire also set the standard for all of the Jewell Dominion guitarists to come. The Jewell Dominion had its beginning in the 1930s and has now embraced three generations and several hundred widely dispersed churches. As the author weaves the story, we discover that the music has largely been transmitted through annual church assemblies, where the music is performed. In the late 1930s, a Gospel Feast Party traveled throughout the eastern United States from New York to Miami, sang, played, preached, and danced. The leader of this group was Reverend J. R. Lockley, and his son, J. R. Jr., played bass, vibraphone, and lap steel guitar at the Church of the Living God's General Assembly all the way through the early 1950s.

Gradually, the steel guitar became the dominant instrument in this idiom. The major figures were treated like rock stars, attracting considerable female attention and drawing appreciative audiences. The author himself spread the news about sacred steel music, through his production of eight sacred steel albums for Arhoolie Records and his documentary video on the subject.

The author describes how Willie Eason developed a technique of imitating the singing voices heard in the churches on the steel guitar. This was an advance from the earlier techniques, where guitarists simply played in a more typical Hawaiian style. Guitarists in both dominions adopted this innovation. Harrison added country and blues guitar influences to the pot, which became accepted in the Jewell Dominion but was frowned upon by the more conservative Keith Dominion. Harrison also utilized tuning variations where the bass strings were pitched as much as an octave below the guitar's low E string.

In Detroit, Keith guitarists Maurice Beard and Calvin Cooke not only brought in new musical influences but also taught students on a regular basis at Beard's church. Stone offers more details on steel guitar–playing techniques and continues the history of the music by discussing modern innovators Chuck Campbell, Glenn Lee, and Robert Randolph. Television appearances and recordings on major labels soon followed. The spread of the music and the pressures on these musicians to establish careers that take them beyond the church subject them to temptations that the conservative nature of these denominations prohibits. The author points out these tensions and contradictions, which certainly parallel some of the same tensions in gospel music.

There are relatively few folk-based styles that have emerged in the twenty-first century. Stone is a reliable guide to the music called "sacred steel." The appendix includes a useful discography and videography.

98. *Traditional and Contemporary Fingerpicking Styles for Guitar.* By Happy Traum. Fortieth anniversary edition. New York: Oak Publications, 2005

This book combines two earlier volumes, which were the first printed methods that taught folk fingerpicking styles. Happy

Traum is a veteran teacher and performer and the owner of Homespun Tapes. That company has produced hundreds of instructional videos, CDs, and instruction books.

The book begins with Traum teaching some basic right-hand techniques. He then defines how picking styles develop out of patterns. After the student has mastered the patterns, the trick is to integrate the melody utilizing aspects of the patterns.

The pieces in this book are by a variety of well-known and less familiar pickers. The author includes outstanding traditional players like Elizabeth Cotten, Etta Baker, and Mississippi John Hurt, but he also has transcribed pieces by younger folk-revival players like Tom Paley, Mike Seeger, and Stefan Grossman. There are even some pieces from players outside the United States. British guitarist Davey Graham's "Angie," as performed by Bert Jansch, is included, as are two African guitar pieces and a piece by the famous Bahamian guitarist Joseph Spence.

There are several ragtime pieces included by revivalist players Eric Schoenberg and Stefan Grossman that require some use of the higher positions on the guitar fingerboard. These are near the end of the book. Because the pieces get progressively more difficult, the player should be able to meet such challenges by that time.

The book includes biographies and photos of the players, and the recordings of the artists are listed on the same page with the music. All pieces are printed in music notation and tablature.

Mastering the styles of so many different artists is a tricky business. Unfortunately, there is no CD included with the book. This requires the reader to buy quite a large group of recordings or to seek out which of these tunes is available on YouTube. This is really a shame, because the book is so good and the tunes are such classic examples of fingerpicking.

Harmonica

99. *Harmonicas, Harps, and Heavy Breathers: The Evolution of the People's Instrument.* By Kim Field. New York: Simon and Schuster, 1993

Rather than trying to write a history of the instrument, Field has compiled an overall analysis of harmonica styles. This is not about folk harmonica per se, but it is an analysis of many styles of harmonica playing.

The author presents the instrument by examining various important players who have developed their own techniques or trademarks. He begins by discussing the pop-vaudeville artists like Borrah Minevitch and the Harmonica Rascals. The next chapter depicts the harmonica soloists, including classical innovator Larry Adler and such pop figures as Richard Hayman and Leo Diamond.

The lengthy sections on folk music, country music, and blues are probably the portions of the book that will be of most interest to readers. In these sections Field traces the development of sound imitations that characterize players like Sonny Terry and Lonnie Glosson. For these players, the sounds of fox chases and railroad trains permeate much of their work.

The blues harmonica then became transmuted into the rock and roll stylings of such artists as Bob Dylan and Lee Oskar. Concluding chapters discuss the use of the harmonica in jazz, notably the work of Toots Thielemans, and its use in Hollywood, as well as such classical players as John Sebastian (Sr.) and Robert Bonfiglio.

Chances are that this book will be most appealing to players of the instrument. There are well-documented discussions of the virtues of the chromatic versus the diatonic harmonica and the specific problems that players have in instrument repair and maintenance. For those with a serious instrument in the lowly "mouth harp," this book is an excellent guide.

Instrumental Collections

100. *Dance to the Fiddle, March to the Fife: Instrumental Folk Tunes in Pennsylvania.* Edited by Samuel P. Bayard. University Park: Pennsylvania State University Press, 1982

Samuel Bayard was a Pennsylvania English professor who collected fiddle and fife tunes throughout his lifetime. The book includes 651 tunes, and the appendix adds forty-four variations of the tunes printed in the body of the text.

In each case, the editor includes the source of the tune and the year in which it was collected. The book incorporates not only Bayard's collecting work but the efforts of three colleagues. Bayard began his collecting work in 1927 and worked without any recording devices until 1948.

The book begins with an introductory section, which discusses the various influences on fiddle tunes, and proceeds to a short section that concerns fiddling technique. The notation is handwritten but is not difficult to read.

Some of the notes on the tunes are short, such as the description of "Lardner's Reel," "This old-fashioned way of playing it." Others contain extensive details about the tunes or the players. All of the sources are listed in the appendix, together with their age and the county where they lived. There is also an extensive bibliography and an index of the tunes.

One of the unusual qualities of this book is that it includes tunes gathered from fife players as well as fiddlers. The author points out that marches were especially suited to fifers, and he also mentions that fife players were virtually extinct by the time his book was published.

This is a unique collection with many unusual tunes as well as some better-known ones. It would have been useful to include guitar chords, but since the author chose to focus on unaccompanied fiddle tunes, it is not surprising that he chose not to include guitar chords.

APPENDIX

A Baker's Dozen of the Next to the Best

ANY SORT OF NUMERICAL LIST INEVITABLY OMITS OTHER WORthy books. Here's a baker's dozen of the next books in line.

1. *The New Song Fest: 300 Songs—Words and Music.* Edited by Dick and Ruth Best. New York: Crown, 1966 (original edition, 1948)

This is a songbook, plain and simple. There are no explanations, no scholarly notes or any other sort of annotations. The editors include the melody lines, guitar chords, and lyrics.

During the early years of the original folk revival, it was this book that was used in campfire sing-alongs, in dormitory parties, and on outings of any kind. An entire generation of singers and guitarists were introduced to folk music through this work. Along with the publisher, the Intercollegiate Outing Club association is credited on the book's cover.

The songs are presented in subject categories, like folksongs and ballads, spirituals, rounds, ski songs, and so on. Although the great majority of the songs are of American origin, there are ten pages of songs from various European countries.

All of the guitar chords listed are quite basic, so even an average guitar player can make his or her way through the book. For its time, this was a pioneering work, and thousands of people learned about folk songs through this book.

This is not a book for the serious folk scholar. There are no discussions of the songs, there are no protest songs, and the book is generally weak on printing African American songs. Nevertheless, thousands of people used this book to learn songs. For anyone who came into the folk revival in the 1940s or 1950s, it is impossible to overlook this work.

2. *Blues Traveling: The Holy Sites of Delta Blues.* By Steve Cheseborough. Third edition. Jackson: University of Mississippi Press, 2009

There is a certain irony to a state like Mississippi creating a tourist industry around the work of musicians who were despised and persecuted in their lifetimes. Having said that, this is, as Tony Joe White put it, "a different place and a different time." Cheseborough offers a comprehensive guide in this book to juke joints, birthplaces, memorials, and museums that commemorate people and events in the blues.

The book is organized by geographical regions, such as Jackson, Clarksdale, and other areas of the state. In each area, Cheseborough lists appropriate matters of interest. The state has actually instituted a blues marker project, erecting signs at points of interest to blues fans and historians. The author is himself a blues performer and has written articles in various blues magazines. As such, he makes a trustworthy guide.

Even though the bulk of the book is centered in Mississippi, the author also has sections on Memphis and Helena, Arkansas. Since many of the Mississippi blues artists gravitated to these towns, especially Memphis, this makes perfect sense. There are maps in some of the sections where the cities are located. Each map marks the spots that would interest a blues tourist, like Furry Lewis's grave in Memphis or the Delta Cultural Center in Helena.

In addition to the sightseeing aspect of the book, radio stations, blues clubs, festivals, recording studios, bookstores, and record shops are listed. Throughout the book are photos of artists and of gravesites and other memorabilia. For the devoted blues fan, archives and museums are listed as well.

From time to time, the author quotes blues lyrics that refer to specific locations. He also offers gastronomical tips for those in search of barbecue or other soul food. Where the sites that he is describing are difficult to locate, Cheseborough gives directions.

This is a unique and satisfying book for the blues aficionado.

3. *Paul Clayton and the Folksong Revival.* By Bob Coltman. Lanham, MD: Scarecrow, 2008

Most of the histories of the folk music revival paint an idyllic picture of folk musicians and folk fans enraptured with roots music and each other. Today Paul Clayton is a footnote to the revival, eclipsed by more popular or more fashionable artists. A sophisticated scholar, a charming raconteur, and a much-recorded singer with a broad repertoire of songs, he would appear to fit comfortably into this stereotype. Coltman reveals that beyond Clayton's scholarly background at the University of Virginia and his log cabin in the wilderness was a tortured soul.

The author sets the table with a brief but excellent discussion of the New York folk scene in the late 1940s and the 1950s and the various folksingers, well known and less famous, who owned the Greenwich Village turf. Clayton was one of the young Turks who came to New York in search of fame and fortune. A few succeeded (can anyone overlook Bob Dylan?). Many retooled their ambitions. Roger Abrahams established a distinguished career as a folklorist, Dave Van Ronk became a Greenwich Village guru, guitar teacher, and performer, Barry Kornfeld became a studio musician, Len Chandler moved to the West Coast and focused on songwriting, and many others simply dropped out of the scene. Clayton belonged to a smaller, less fortunate group. Like Peter La Farge and Phil Ochs, his personal demons combined with the pressure of competing with Bob Dylan and surviving in a very tough music industry reduced him to extensive drug and alcohol use and ultimately, as with the others, to suicide. As Coltman documents, Clayton bore the additional cross of being, depending on one's view, gay or bisexual at a time when even in the Village this was not considered to be "cool."

It seems that in Clayton's case, as well as with Phil Ochs, a great deal of energy and time was devoted to obtaining the approval of Bob Dylan, the obvious if not appointed king of folk. In Ochs's case, Dylan directly critiqued his songwriting, dismissing him as a journalist, not a songwriter. As Coltman tells the story, Clayton was enamored, possibly literally and figuratively, with Dylan. Dylan reworked a Clayton rearrangement of a folk song into "Don't Think Twice, It's All Right," and eventually his publisher bought Clayton off for five hundred dollars. This for a song that by this time has undoubtedly earned well over a million dollars. Yet Clayton continued to defer to Dylan, went on an extensive road trip with him, and then eventually fell out of the Dylan orbit, as so many of Dylan's early associates did.

The author has brilliantly brought to bear the underbelly of the folk revival, the backbiting, the quest for fame and fortune, and the difficulties of maintaining friendships. The irony of it all is that today Clayton might well have thrived as a house concert artist. He was charming, handsome, and before his self-abuse became intense, an excellent storyteller who charmed small audiences. He simply wasn't suited to the "big stage," not as a recording artist or as a performer. Coltman is generous in assessing Clayton's importance, possibly a bit too much so. The lyrics published in the appendix reveal that other than his co-writing of the song "Gotta Travel On," Clayton was a lyricist of average talent whose Bob Dylan worship and influence overwhelmed his own abilities.

Anyone with a serious interest in the folk revival can benefit from reading this book because it is so good at revealing the contradictions between the mystique of folk music and the ways that folksingers tried to survive in the music industry.

4. *Steve Goodman: Facing the Music.* By Clay Eels. Toronto: ECW Press, third printing, 2012

This is a lengthy autobiography of Steve Goodman, a singer-songwriter who lived half of his life, and virtually *all* of his adult life, under a death sentence from leukemia.

To the extent that Goodman is known, it is because he was the author of "City of New Orleans," a major hit record by Arlo Guthrie that was also recorded by Willie Nelson, John Denver, and numerous other artists. In his native Chicago, Goodman was also known for writing several songs about the hapless Chicago White Sox, and in the world of country music, he achieved some popularity with his song "You Never Even Called Me by My Name," written with his friend John Prine and recorded by David Allan Coe.

Goodman's life, and to some extent this book, are both a mass of contradictions. This book is twice as long as Joe Klein's biography of Woody Guthrie or David Dunaway's biography of Pete Seeger. With no offense intended toward Goodman, does the importance of his contributions merit such a lengthy tome? The answer is going to depend partly on the reader's interest in his compelling life story and whether the reader is attached to the Chicago portion of the folk music revival. This book is certainly the most detailed treatment of the Chicago scene, and as such is a valuable corrective to the constant emphasis on New York in books about the folk music revival.

As for the contradictions in Goodman's own life, the author doesn't really deal with the contradiction between Goodman's musical values and his striving for commercial success with what seem to frequently turn out to be ill-fated commercial music ventures. Many questions are left unanswered. Why wasn't the author able to interview Goodman's mother, his wife, his brother, and only one of his three daughters? What Eels has done is to substitute a mind-bending number of interviews with Goodman's friends and associates, musical associates, his manager, Al Bunetta, and friends dating back to Goodman's childhood.

Goodman is one among several singer-songwriters, notably Tim Hardin and Fred Neil, whose fame came from hit recordings of their songs by other artists. Why success eluded Goodman as an artist is not clear from this biography. By all accounts, Goodman was a wonderful live entertainer. Five of his recordings were on the Asylum label, the home of such successful singer-songwriters as Joni Mitchell and Jackson Browne. Yet his earlier records on disco label Buddah were actually more successful in terms of the number of albums sold, about fifty thousand at the maximum. It wasn't a matter of exposure, because during his tenure at Asylum, he opened two hundred shows for a then-rising comic named Steve Martin.

I have included this book because of Goodman's compelling life story and the details it offers about the folk scene in Chicago and because in many ways it highlights the way the music business dealt with everything except folksong superstars. In many ways, the book raises far more questions than it answers. Less concentration on specific gigs and so many names that will mean little or nothing to most readers and more attention to the questions that I have raised here might have made this compelling story more readable and guaranteed it a wider audience. Downloads of eighteen tracks with songs written and performed by other artists in tribute to Steve Goodman are available free with the book.

5. *Blind but Now I See: The Biography of Music Legend Doc Watson.* By Kent Gustavson. New York: Bloomington Twig Books, 2010

Doc Watson is one of the most important acoustic guitarists of the twentieth century. This book is a biography of Doc with considerable attention devoted to his musical career.

Gustavson casts considerable light on Doc Watson's character. I suppose he could be described as a person who continually wrestled with contradictory currents. A master of acoustic guitar and a student of traditional music, Watson was playing a Les Paul solid-body electric guitar in a rockabilly band when folklorists "discovered" him. Anxious to please his parents and blind from birth, Watson attended a school for the blind for four years until he virtually refused to return. A shy, reserved man, Watson became a superb performer, much in demand from audiences with whom he had little in common.

The book points out many of these contradictions. Among its most interesting insights is the way that urban folk revivalists/folk song collectors like Ralph Rinzler attempted to manipulate the repertoire of their discoveries. This was done in the interests of maintaining the image of purity that acoustic music represented to these collectors.

What is left for the reader to guess at is the question of what right these urban products had to determine the question of valid repertoire. Moreover, the collectors discussed in some detail, Rinzler and John Cohen, were both urban, college-educated products.

As we follow Watson going through the rigors of his performing career, we see him trying to make a living for his family and enduring the loss of his son Merle. The author takes us into the orbit of Watson's life and family, and we are left with the sadness and sense of loss that came from the senseless, if somewhat controversial, nature of Merle's death.

If you play guitar and you haven't heard Doc Watson, you owe it to yourself to get one or more of his albums. I would have welcomed the author's paying a bit more attention to the nature of Watson's wonderful crosspicking technique. Ralph Rinzler died before Gustavson completed his book, but it would have been useful if the author had posed some difficult questions to John Cohen and the various other New York revival promoters, the Friends of Old-Time Music, on the nature of purity and authenticity.

6. *Ten Thousand Goddam Cattle: A History of the American Cowboy in Song, Story and Verse.* By Katie Lee. Albuquerque: University of New Mexico Press, third printing, revised, 1985

This entertaining book revolves around the author's long-term search for the town of Delores, portrayed in a song by James Grafton Rogers. Katie Lee is a nightclub performer and long-time aficionado of cowboy songs. The book includes not only her quest to discover whether Delores was an actual town, but sojourns with such cowboys and songwriters as Shorty Bob, Gail Gardner, and Jenny Wells Vincent.

I wouldn't call this book a scholarly work so much as a work of scholarship. It includes the melody line, words, and chords for a number of songs. Some are well known, many are obscure, to say the least. Lee includes them either because she likes the informants or the songs have some specific significance. She also means to highlight the real life of the working cowboy as opposed to his Hollywood counterpart.

Along the way, we learn a good deal about how songs circulate and in some cases how the author loses financial and literary control over her own creations. Gardner himself is a cowboy who earned a BS in mathematics from Dartmouth but returned to his western home to become an Arizona rancher. Lee includes an extensive description of Gardner's song "The Sierry Petes." A cowboy friend of his called the Sierra Peaks the Sierra Petes. Lee herself has heard the song performed as "The Frisco Peaks," "The Chirichua Peaks," "Dragoon Peaks," and "Mountain Peaks." This is an excellent case study of how a song that enters the tradition is transformed by various performers or informants. Lee plays Gardner a version of the song sung by folksinger Rosalie Sorrels, and Gardner points out how various words that had specific meanings get changed by artists or performers who are not themselves cowboys or cowgirls. There are also stories about how other artists claimed the song, including Peter La Farge and Powder River Jack. Later in the book, Lee describes how Powder River Jack and some other New York and Chicago "song pulps" took cowboy poems and songs and copyrighted them under their own names. Lee compares the WLS Barn Dance and Opry performers with actual cowboys, pointing out that the cowboys were concerned with a sense of place, not simply the words and music. She does credit a few later artists, like Steve Fromholz and Travis Edmonsen, as delivering an accurate vision of western balladry.

At the end of the book, Lee finally succeeds in her fool's quest and finds there was indeed a town called Delores, in New Mexico. Along the way, we have all discovered quite a few matters about cowboy songs and the people who wrote them. Some readers will find Lee's attitudes about cowboys, dudes, and tourists subjective and occasionally unfair. I think that most readers will be entertained by her no-nonsense style and opinions.

> 7. *Hard Hitting Songs for Hard-Hit People.* Compiled by Alan Lomax. Notes on the songs by Woody Guthrie. Music transcribed and edited by Pete Seeger. New York: Oak Publications, 1967

This book originated in the mind of Alan Lomax in the late 1930s, but he couldn't find a publisher, World War II then happened, and the book became a manuscript sitting in the People's Song Library. Irwin Silber found it in 1961 in a disorganized form until a carbon copy was turned up by John Cohen. He got it through his brother, Mike, from Liz Ambellan, whose ex-husband had it. He had a downtown loft, and Woody had stayed there sometimes and had probably left the book there.

This is an interesting book with easy-to-use lead sheets that contain melodies and chords. There are many great blues, some well-known songs, some obscure ones, and a good selection from the Kentucky mining protest group—Aunt Molly Jackson, her half-sister Sara Ogan, her brother Jim Garland, and others.

Woody Guthrie's introductions to the songs are written in his rambling, folksy style and after a while become a bit of an albatross. It might have been better to have specific details about the composers or the songs themselves. As it is, what we get is a generous sprinkling of Woody's folksy autobiography and his personal slant on things. Some of the songs were collected by the WPA, for example, "Those Old Cumberland Mountain Farms." There are lots of John and Alan Lomax copyrights here. Because Alan Lomax had an excellent collection of blues recordings, there are quite a few blues here. There are also some Leadbelly numbers and a number of Guthrie songs, both little and well known. There are also some songs of the Wobblies (Industrial Workers of the World), songs from the Dust Bowl, and some of John Handcox's tunes. Handcox was a black worker who was involved in union organizing and some Socialist Party work. Oddly, despite the many words from Woody, there is no biographical information on Handcox here.

All in all, this is a very useful book and a good companion for Greenway's *American Folksongs of Protest* (no. 74). There is also a bit too much of Woody running off at the mouth here. It is unclear what Lomax contributed beyond his record collection. This is another book that manages to entirely ignore the work of Lawrence Gellert. One wonders whether this is a reflection of ignorance or of the somewhat frosty relationship between Gellert and the Lomaxes.

8. *The Denver Folk Music Tradition: An Unplugged History, from Harry Tuft to Swallow Hill and Beyond.* By Paul Malkoski. Charleston, SC: History Press, 2012

This book is the only one that deals with an acoustic music store, its founder, and a nonprofit organization that has grown into a major teaching facility and concert venue.

Malkoski begins the story with the arrival of Harry Tuft, founder of the Denver Folklore Center, in Denver. It then weaves his story into the emergence of the acoustic music scene in Denver in the early 1960s. Most of the books about the folk music revival either ignore the importance of music shops as community gathering places or focus almost entirely on Israel Young's Folklore Center in New York. Although Young certainly deserves that attention, there were at least a half-dozen stores that provided a similar function in the revival.

Harry Tuft's story is probably somewhat typical of the founders of these stores. Harry was (and is) a part-time musician who managed to integrate his notion of community service and his musical interests into providing himself with the ability to make a living in a music-related enterprise. The author shows how Harry started with almost no merchandise and even lived in a loft in his own store for several years.

The original location of the store, six blocks east of downtown Denver, was a neighborhood that provided low-rent housing to a mixed community of minority group members and hippies. As was the case with so many of the proprietors of acoustic music stores, Harry found himself in the concert business. A small, single store developed into an entire small block of related enterprises, including a record store, a used clothing shop, a repair shop, a music store, and a concert hall. By 1980, the store closed down and moved under new management to another location. When that store failed, in 1983, Harry, along with a group of other folk music fans, began to organize a music organization called the Music Association of Swallow Hill.

The second half of Malkoski's book is devoted to Swallow Hill. It is a fascinating story, replete with changes of leadership, rethinking of the role of the board of directors, and the purchase of a stand-alone facility with three performance spaces and many teaching rooms. Along the way there were various conflicts between the employees and board members in regard to the balance of concerts and teaching. As seems to be the case with other similar facilities, the teaching aspect of the business brings in positive cash flow, while the concert business tends to be a break-even matter or a loss leader. The argument, which Malkoski presents, is that it is the concerts that bring in fresh faces who later become students at the school.

Because I have a minor role in this story, there are some errors in the book that I discovered. Harry Tuft never performed at the hungry i in San Francisco but at a coffeehouse called the Fox and the Hounds. David Ferretta's music store was not called the Global Village but Ferretta Music. The Global Village was another enterprise, a coffee shop with a performance space that Ferretta owned. Although the author acknowledges the influence of the Folklore Center in New York, he fails to mention McCabe's in Los Angeles-Santa Monica. (The Folklore Center opened in 1957, McCabe's in 1958.) The WOW Hall in Eugene in fact presents very little folk music today but concentrates on alternative rock, with occasional world music and singer-songwriters. Finally, the conflict between the former school administrator and concert hall director is presented in considerable detail. However, the author doesn't seem to have interviewed the concert director to get her side of the story. If she was unwilling to talk to him, that information should appear in the book.

Denver remains a hotbed of acoustic music, and as the author points out, Harry Tuft reopened his Folklore Center in a new location in 1992. For anyone interested in acoustic music and the acoustic music community, this book plays an important role in capturing that magic.

9. *Singing Soldiers.* By John J. Niles. New York: Charles Scribner's Sons, 1927

John Jacob Niles had a long and colorful career as a folk music collector, performer, and songwriter who did not initially acknowledge that some of his songs were composed by him. He served in the American air force in 1917 and, inspired by a volume of French war songs, decided to collect a similar group of songs from American soldiers. Initially, he collected from white soldiers. World War I was the first war where African Americans served in large numbers, but they were in segregated units. Frustrated with the results of his efforts with white soldiers, who were mostly singing songs by professional songwriters, Niles turned to black companies. Here he found a veritable harvest of original songs. Since he

was serving as a pilot, Niles made his way into virtually every
area occupied by American troops.

Among his many adventures, Niles organized a black-
face minstrel show. Musically, what he found in his labors was
an interesting basket of songs. Going through the pages of
Singing Soldiers, you find new versions of spirituals, improvisa-
tions, call-and-response-pattern songs, and laments of loneli-
ness. Niles notated all of the songs except on the occasions
where he was too tired or had enjoyed a few too many liba-
tions to remain entirely rational.

Among the sort of improvised songs that Niles found are
a song that was a tongue-in-cheek tribute to a French railroad
man, "Forty eight men and eight army horses, Goin' to come
back home wid some nice German crosses," or another song,
"The Soldier Man Blues," which starts out with "I got de mean
man, movin' van, yellow dog wid a can, Holy hell, soldier man
blues."

One soldier, known as the Chicken Butcher, exhibits
some of the rambling, loose-life traits that Howard Odum and
Guy Johnson (no. 61) found in their informant Left Wing
Gordon.

Without Niles's book, we would have only the sketchi-
est knowledge of what songs black soldiers were singing in
1917–1918. Given Niles's predilection for recomposition, it is
difficult to know whether the melodies printed are precisely
the ones he heard, but in any case this book opens a window
to the process of creation and improvisation in black music
in 1917–1918. This was a period when very few black secular
songs had appeared in print, so Niles has preserved something that would likely have been lost forever to future generations. This book is out of print and is most likely to be found
in large libraries.

10. *Ragtime for Fiddle & Mandolin.* By Stephen C. Parker. Edited by Alan Davis. Los Angeles: Steve Parker Music, 2006

Ragtime became popular at the turn of the twentieth century, roughly at the time the blues surfaced. Steve Parker has arranged 124 tunes for fiddle and mandolin with guitar chords.

Everything is written out in very readable standard music notation, but there is no tablature in this book. The music could also conceivably be played on banjo or guitar, although it would require some adaptation by the player to make the music work in the different tunings that those instruments use. A CD in MP3 format contains all of the tunes in the book. This is useful in terms of accuracy and essential if you have mediocre music-reading skills.

The tunes represent a treasure trove of ragtime style. Some of the music comes from such well-known acoustic musicians as Chet Atkins and Mike Seeger. Others come from recordings by groups like the Dallas String Band and folk revival players like Brad Leftwich, and some go back to the late 1890s, like "At a Georgia Camp Meeting" by Kerry Mills.

Biographies, photos, and drawings of famous players festoon the book throughout. The tunes themselves vary from little-known turn-of-the-century favorites to folk-revival staples like "Beaumont Rag."

There are numerous collections of fiddle tunes arranged for fiddle, mandolin, and guitar. This is the most comprehensive book that I have encountered of ragtime tunes. Since many of these tunes are little known and a bit more difficult to master than the tunes found in such collections, playing through this book makes for an excellent learning experience.

11. *The Great Folk Discography: Pioneers & Early Legends.* By Martin C. Strong. Edinburgh: Polygon, 2010

In general, I have avoided including books that are primarily marketed in the United Kingdom in this work. *The Great Folk Discography,* however, is such a massive and unique guide that I feel it is worthy of inclusion here. It contains over six hundred pages of discographical data. There are over three hundred pages devoted to American recordings, followed by 270 pages that list British recordings and an additional twenty-six pages devoted to "cult, collectable and continental" recordings.

Each listing is preceded by a description of the artist and the artist's music. The author's notion of "folk" is clearly governed by what I like to call folk-based music. In other words, if a listing of recordings by the Jefferson Airplane or the Lovin' Spoonful offends you, this is not a book that you will enjoy. I presume that part of the author's logic in including these groups is that many of the members of the band had a considerable background in acoustic music and in some cases continue to play it today.

For each recording listed, the author includes the label name, the date of the album release, the format (LP, CD, etc.), and the catalog number of the release. In cases where the album appeared on pop charts, the chart position in the United Kingdom or United States is listed.

Strong's descriptions of the artists are generally fair-minded, and he includes information about what happened to the artist after the listed albums were released. Since many of the artists were in groups that disbanded in a relatively short period of time, this enables the reader to find out what the artist did after leaving the group.

Occasionally credits listed for the artists are not entirely accurate but appear to have come from PR material spun by the artists. This is a small price to pay for such an overwhelming project.

12. *Puro Conjunto: An Album in Words & Pictures.* Edited by Juan Tejeda and Avelardo Valdez. San Antonio: Guadalupe Cultural Center, 2001

Most of the books about the music of the Mexican border focus on specific song types, such as *corridos* or *narcocorridos.* This book is a collection of articles by various writers, detailing the history and development of *conjunto* music in the twentieth century.

The articles cover a broad overview of Tejano music. The subject matter includes accordion styles, a history of the *bajo sexto* (the Mexican version of the twelve-string guitar), interviews with such key artists as Santiago Jiménez Sr. and Valerio Longorio, and observations, histories, and opinions about the social and political history of the music.

Juan Tejeda, one of the editors, is the founder of the annual Texas Conjunto Festival in San Antonio, and he has included seventeen colorful posters from that festival. There are also black-and-white photos of many of the artists discussed in the text. All in all, there are thirty-three contributions by twenty-four authors.

A number of controversial matters are discussed in the text. Some of the authors see the commercialization of the music as detrimental to it, while others see hybridization as a positive cultural force. Flaco Jiménez, the son of Santiago Jiménez Sr., has achieved popularity far beyond the Mexican American community through his appearances on recordings by Anglo artists Paul Simon and Ry Cooder. Some of the older musicians interviewed felt that this exposure removed him from the community, while others thought that these activities brought a new level of respect for and interest in their music.

The article about the lack of women musicians in the music is particularly revealing. It raises issues of family and tradition and discusses how the lifestyle of working musicians tends to erode the traditional family structure. The Guadalupe Cultural Arts Center has made instruction in *conjunto* music feasible in a nonthreatening environment that is somewhat removed from sexism and stereotypical images of women.

A final chapter distinguishes *conjunto* from the Tejano orchestra. Tejano music features accordion, *bajo sexto*, bass, and drums, while the *orquestra Tejano* is modeled after the big bands of the swing era, with horns, piano, and/or guitar.

The article about celebrated accordion player Valerio Longorio describes how he was paid the minuscule sum of fifteen dollars for recording two songs. The parallel to the way many blues artists were treated is unmistakable, although the authors do not discuss this. I was a bit surprised that the book never mentions the American Federation of Musicians Tejano Star Movement (Support Tejano Musicians in Recording). This movement, designed to improve the working condition of Tejano recording musicians, started in 1997.

During the 1990s *Westword*, a local weekly, did a special inserted section of the paper on Mexican American music in Denver. I was amazed to find that I knew virtually none of the artists listed or the venues that they played in, although I had been playing music professionally in the area for twenty years. I suspect that many of the readers of this book are in the same position. This book will prove an excellent guide for them.

13. *Leadbelly*. By Tyehimba Jess. Amherst, MA: Verso Press, 2005

Tyehimba's work is a book of poems about Huddie (Leadbelly) Ledbetter, the great African American songster.

I have included this book because it details Leadbelly's adult life. Jess uses an inventive combination of his own poems, song lyrics, and letters from Leadbelly. He also includes letters from John Lomax and from Josh White. In the case of the various letters, the back of the book includes specific references for the letters.

In many ways, this book is an interesting supplement to the Charles Wolfe-Kip Lornell biography of Leadbelly (no. 19). Because Jess is writing a work of poetry, he weaves poetic visions of Leadbelly's life as a convict, his love life, and his relationship with John Lomax into the book.

Readers who are unaware of the complex and sometimes exploitative relationship between John Lomax and Leadbelly may be startled by Jess's description of Lomax coming to Angola prison where the author, speaking in the convict's voice, says "he wants the secret of cockwalk in the chords." This reveals the ambivalence of the southern-raised Lomax about Leadbelly's power and sexuality.

Lomax fans and supporters may also be offended by Leadbelly's reflection that

> you pick up the pen, and when you put it down again
> you are two thirds less than what you started with.
> one third the man your father raised you to be.

This refers to Leadbelly's relatively prosperous father and the percentage of his own earnings that the singer paid to the Lomaxes. Initially the amount was 50 percent, but when John Lomax recruited his son Alan, who apparently had better rapport with Leadbelly, they raised their commission to two-thirds.

This is an innovative book that explores the relationship between poetry and music while at the same time painting a portrait of the artist and his somewhat futile attempts to succeed in the world of music. The only missing piece of the puzzle is the relationship between Alan Lomax and the singer.

INDEX

ABOUT THE AUTHOR

Dick Weissman is a musician, composer, and folk music performer who has been active in various aspects of the folk music revival. He has written or coauthored nineteen books about music and the music industry, including *Which Side Are You On? An Inside History of the Folk Revival*, which was a finalist for the Oregon Book Award in nonfiction writing in 2006, and *The Folk Music Sourcebook*, coauthored with Larry Sandberg. The latter book won the ASCAP Deems Taylor Music Critics Award in 1977. He is an associate professor emeritus in the Music & Entertainment Industry program at the University of Colorado at Denver and an adjunct professor at Portland Community College, Cascade Campus.